A Trip to the Tip

Also by Steven Cavini and published by Ginninderra Press
Natalia: Her life, her family, her tragedy

Steven Cavini

A Trip to the Tip

A Trip to the Tip
ISBN 978 1 76109 688 4
Copyright © text Cavini 2024

First published 2024 by
GINNINDERRA PRESS
PO Box 3461 Port Adelaide 5015
www.ginninderrapress.com.au

Contents

Foreword	7
Seeking Utopia	9
Port Albert	14
Melbourne	17
Day 1	19
Day 2	23
Day 3	28
Day 4	31
Day 5	34
Day 6	37
Day 7	41
Day 8	46
Day 9	49
Day 10	53
Day 11	57
Day 12	64
Day 13	66
Day 14	69
Day 15	73
Day 16	75
Day 17	78
Day 18	87
Day 19	94
Day 20	97
Day 21	99
Day 22	104

Day 23	108
Day 24	114
Day 25	117
Day 26	118
Day 27	121
Day 28	122
Day 29	124
Day 30	127
Day 31	130
Day 32	132
Day 33	135
Day 34	139
Day 35	142
Day 36	145
Day 37	147
Day 38	148
Day 39	153
Day 40	156
Day 41	157
Day 42	158
Day 43–Day 47	162
Day 48	166
Day 49	167
Day 50	168
Day 51	170
Day 52	171
Day 53	174
Home	176
Epilogue	179

Foreword

I am sure that many of you recall trips to the tip, where, perhaps for the price of a rusty nail piercing one's sole, any scavenger worth his or her salt could strike gold. Perhaps as a child with your father, most likely, or maybe with your mother, or both; searching for nuggets amongst the tailings of civilised living. Perhaps as a young adult with things to be built or an old house to be renovated; trying to save a dollar or two as well as creating something with a fashionably rustic look. Perhaps as a parent with your own kids now, introducing them to the delight of scavenging as you search for parts for a cubby house or billy-cart.

Alas, in most places now these wondrous experiences have gone the way of so many others: no longer permitted. As we have moved from the tip to the grandiose-sounding transfer stations and recycling depots, the ultimate expression of recycling, and a way for the battler to save some dough, has been curtailed. Today, we must shell out for everything and buy new stuff when old would do, just for it to end up decrepit and in the transfer station just as surely as we are to one day die, for the second law of thermodynamics says it must be so. We are all destined for the recycling depot.

I fear that this inability to scavenge is yet another source of the unhappiness that seems to prevail amongst humans nowadays. We are forced to go to Bunnings rather than experiencing the fun and satisfaction of a trip to the tip. Getting something we need, for nothing, is a small win against the perpetual grind of an ungenerous world in which every dollar counts; and it makes us happy, like vultures at a carcass, and yet it is increasingly denied to us.

But all of that is merely an aside. None of the above is in any way relevant to this book; I simply wanted to get that off my chest by using an embarrassingly simple play on words. So do not concern yourselves, my friends, for this book has nothing whatsoever to do with the type of tip I have just described, fond as I was of them, but rather deals with one of an entirely different nature, one perhaps of even more interest depending on one's outlook: a trip to the tip of Cape York no less!

Wow, that's more like it, I hear some of you exclaim, with a mixture of excitement and relief. Why bother, I hear others grizzle – the stay-at-homes who gather moss and would not even join a gold rush at gunpoint. I hope that this book will further amaze those in the first category just as I was so often amazed, for it is a wonderful thing at any age to still have the capacity and the opportunity to be amazed. To those in the second category, who are unlikely to pick up and read this book anyway unless under the erroneous impression that it really does mean a nostalgic trip to the local dumping ground to get free stuff, I sincerely hope that this work answers the question of 'why bother?' even if they never get to go there themselves.

Finally, I beg your indulgence for I have a cautionary word to the prospective reader. If you are looking for a nuts-and-bolts travel guide which includes all the attractions, where to eat, motel prices and all that other boring stuff that does my head in, then this book isn't for you. It is a work which includes my own itinerary and observations and thoughts, some sensible and some deranged, the latter including some of the bizarre things which came to mind as I spent idle hours behind the wheel. And I hope you will also forgive my self-indulgence, for I have thrown in the occasional non-poet's poem for good measure in the sincere hope that they will not induce true poets out there to reach for a plastic bag.

Factual content came partly from my own rather feeble brain but mostly from local information signs and pamphlets as well as references from Wikipedia and other sources which I have referenced at the time.

So, read on, my friends, if your are willing and fit to dare.

Seeking Utopia

Utopia, utopia...
Where can I find ya?

It is said that the beginning is a good place at which to begin but, in an act akin to fathoming the precursor to the big bang, I would like to instead begin before the beginning, way back to when I met my partner.

I found her in Essendon, as I drove along Keilor Road, standing in a car yard but, as far as I could tell, not looking at anything at all but merely staring straight ahead, as if afflicted with tunnel vision. To me, she appeared more like a trophy on a pedestal than just a trophy. Her appeal was instantaneous and indomitable. She looked so young and fresh and gleaming and beautiful and glorious. I decided there and then that I would join up with her and we did in fact do that a mere few weeks later, in 2005, after a courtship involving some negotiation and substantial expense.

I never feared for a moment that she would not be worth every cent and that faith I had in her was vindicated many times over. She worked incredibly hard on the farm, every bit as hard as I did, and often harder, without complaint and never letting me down. And here we are seventeen years later, with the farm long gone, still together, happy, making a new life, and she looks every bit as good as she did back then; almost. How many men can say that about their partner without a word of it being a lie?

A few years ago, I decided that a holiday would be good for both of us, after so many years of unrelenting toil, and she made no objection when I suggested a trip to the Cape, even though it would be a rough and dusty journey with few comforts. She isn't one for comforts and I, too, can do without them for some time. The idea was nascent of a desire on my part to eventually visit all four extremities of the mainland

and as I had already visited the most southerly and easterly, all that remained were the more challenging and distant north and west.

My partner responded in her typical way by not responding at all but I did not think it odd, it was simply her way; work or pleasure was all the same to her. So it was decided: a trip to the tip of Cape York and back would become a reality in 2020, but then Covid intervened and the plans were filed away until, in 2022, Australia opened up again and it was time to move.

I have, at this point, a confession to make; I know next to nothing about cars and I haven't done much four-wheel driving and absolutely none of the more serious kind. Sure, I can check the oil and water and change a flat tyre, I can tell the front from the back and the driver's side from the passenger's, and just like everyone else I think I am the best driver going round and that no one else is quite up to the mark but that is about as far as it goes. So, in my ignorance, the idea of having a car break down in the middle of nowhere has always been an irritant in my side and a reason for postponement.

The key, as I saw it, was preparation so, to avoid just such a calamity as far as it is possible necessitated some works on the car, a '98 Land Cruiser cab chassis with a tipping tray which had been ideal on the farm and would be just as ideal for rough terrestrial travelling. She is the best thing I have ever bought, as well as the most enduring and, as I have already mentioned, she has never complained and never let me down. I love her dearly and I earnestly hope that our partnership will endure to my dying day and that when that day finally arrives, she will carry my coffin to the graveside and tip me straight into the hole in the ground. Wouldn't that be something to behold.

The initial planning for this trip goes back many years to when I had a neighbour, who is very clever with a mig, weld up a cage that could be bolted onto her tray. Then I had a canvas cover with zip-up sides, made locally in Wodonga, that fitted snugly over the cage so that, when the time for travel finally came, the home was ready, like a snail's, and all that was needed were the furnishings.

Three years ago, I bought a second spare wheel and an emergency puncture repair thing that works in mysterious ways but has directions attached.

Two years ago, I found out that one of the leaf springs was cracked so I took her to a place to get it fixed and ended up getting the entire suspension replaced and the steering fixed, whether it really needed it or not. Who's to know? Sometimes, ignorance forces you into situations of blind trust and into the realm of gut feelings but I soothed the pain of the cost with comforting thoughts that she was old and that she had done a lot of hard yakka, so it probably was necessary to get the repairs done. And besides, I said to myself, it amounted to two less things that could go wrong when I was 'out there', in the 'never-never', where something going wrong with the car can result in one becoming skeletonised and desiccated in some far-flung outpost of the outback.

One year ago, on the advice of a Toyota mechanic who I really do trust, I had the radiator replaced and, with that, another possible source of disaster was averted.

Finally, just before the start of the trip, she had her 250,000-kilometre service and the brakes redone. The latter, I'm sure, did indeed send disaster packing when it came courting. All that work and cost was very reassuring and made me confident that she could get me there and back without a hitch. What is more, she never complained once despite the intrusive nature of the procedures and the costs involved.

I'm so proud of my partner. She doesn't nag with alarms and flashing lights and sensors like the young 'uns do nowadays. She's old-school, just like me, which is perhaps why our partnership has endured for so long. Being technologically simple and not too smart, lacking all the whizz-bang computers and electronics and all that razzamatazz, makes her very easy to deal with. She has manual transmission and manually operated windows and you actually have to get off your arse and get out to free or lock the front wheels and I love her all the more for those ancient and, dare I say, even quaint features.

But, alas, perfection is nowhere to be found, not even in my sweetheart. I do have a grizzle, only one, which is her capacity to guzzle. She loves a drink, always has, and she steadfastly refuses to admit to being a dieselholic. She stubbornly refuses to reduce her consumption no matter how much I try to talk to her and counsel her and complain. In that respect, she is a lot like most other cars, and people for that matter – very set in her ways.

With departure a matter of days away, it was time to get serious. I put the toolbox in order so that it consisted of the RACV phone number (with top roadside assistance paid up), a jack, a wheelbrace, a tow chain, a screwdriver (not sure what type, whether flathead or Philips, nor where it was exactly) and an adjustable spanner. I forgot the jumper leads. I bought a couple of jerrycans for fuel and a twenty-litre plastic container to add to a ten-litre one I already had for water.

Then I had to get the home in order: bedding, storage and kitchen. The back is quite spacious, the tray being larger than standard size, having been enlarged to the specifications of Darebin Council parks and gardens' requirements. To store stuff, I used a small cupboard given to me by my niece, Natalie, which has top and bottom compartments and which fitted perfectly within the tray when placed on its side. I stored pots, pans, billies, cups and cutlery on one side and food on the other. I used a cardboard box for miscellaneous stuff.

Bedding consisted of two self-inflating mattresses taped together for extra luxury, two pillows, a sheet, a thin doona, and a down bag to throw over for the extra chilly nights. It was cosy and very comfortable but prone to getting gritty and grimy.

The kitchen consisted of two nine-kilo 'swap 'n' goes' and a gas burner; simple yet versatile. Clothes I kept in a travel case on the passenger seat. The other stuff went wherever: shoes, boots, thongs, hats, toiletries, pills, towels, sunblock, lanterns, repellent, mosquito netting, et cetera.

With so much to do, the final days slipped by easily, like good whisky down a gullet, barely noticed until, before I knew it, all was in readiness and it was time to go. I said my goodbyes to three dogs: Boof,

Joe and Utah, whose names are in alphabetical order so as not to cause anyone offence, as well as to several people: Alexis, Frank and Jani, Jenny, Murray and Norma, and Stephen, also, you may have observed, in alphabetical order. Through my life, and my various lives, I have found, often to my chagrin, that people can be easily offended and angered, even over the most inane trivialities. I have learnt from such unsettling occurrences and have, in time, made adjustments in an attempt to live the years I have left to me as peacefully as possible while, at the same time, not being a doormat. It is a fine line to tread.

My first task before setting off on my quest for utopia was to give the old girl a good scrub and polish so that she sparkled like an ageless jewel in the sun.

Port Albert

Port Albert, you are so fine.
I'll be back in but a short time.
Your wares are the best
But your winters do test.
In your bosom I will gladly do the other nine.

I fixed my departure day from my recently adopted hometown for the 29 June 2022 so as to be in Melbourne the following day for my sister's birthday.

For those who don't know, Port Albert is a small seaside town in eastern Victoria, just south of Yarram, east of Wilson's Promontory and near the start of the Ninety Mile Beach, which makes it amongst the most southerly towns on the Australian mainland, hence making my journey to the tip of Cape York almost as far south to north as it is possible to go. My travels would far exceed the south to north distance covered by Burke and Wills (and King and Gray) but then I do have certain advantages which they lacked back in 1861 and which I hoped would see me through to its finale, alive and in one piece.

Yearning both to live by the sea and for a cooler climate, but with economics also being a major consideration, I moved to the area two years ago and into the town just a few months ago. Sheltered as its waters are by a series of sand islands from the fury of Bass Strait, it was Gippsland's first port, established in 1841 to serve local farms and thriving pastoralists but it was during the gold rush that Port Albert boomed. Miners and their supplies disembarked here, bound for Walhalla, Jericho, Dargo and Crooked River. Gold was taken by ship back to Melbourne.

Port Albert's decline came with the arrival of the railway to Gippsland and it is now a quiet town steeped in history and with several surviving colonial buildings adding their period charm to the place. It has a population of around three hundred and relies on fishing and tourism to keep it ticking over but its decline continues, particularly with the loss in 2014 of its iconic hotel to fire and just recently with the closure of several businesses further threatening its tenuous hold on prosperity.

Despite all that, it is the perfect place for me at this stage of my life. I welcome its tranquillity and there remains a beating heart within its community which, though surely to be tested in the years to come, will just as surely endure, for its charms are many and varied. Its waterways, foreshore and jetties are delightful. The old wharf area is historic and now dominated by majestic Norfolk Island pines. The local maritime museum and art gallery are full of wonders. But for me it is the natural beauty that really shines. Vast areas of mangrove mudflats dominate, barely touched since the arrival of white man. Important areas of seagrass provide a nursery for many types of fish which in turn support important colonies of seabirds including migratory visitors from as far away as Siberia. Large areas including the offshore islands are protected by the Nooramunga Marine Park. I can think of few things more pleasing than to walk along Port Albert's foreshore on a sunny day when the wind grants a brief reprieve.

The town was named, in the patriotic past, after Prince Albert, Queen Victoria's husband as well as a great man in his own right, whose premature death she mourned for the rest of her life. I am pleased to live in a town that bears his name, for he championed the cause of anti-slavery, was a keen patron of the arts, took a keen and intelligent interest in technological advancements and was a prime mover in bringing the Crystal Palace and the Great Exhibition of London in 1851 to fruition.

The exhibition turned out to be a huge success both in terms of international prestige as well as financially, in no small part because of Prince Albert's efforts, and the profits generated were used to build the

Royal Albert Hall, the Imperial College London, the Victoria and Albert Museum, the Science Museum and the Natural History Museum.

For a time, he was also chancellor of Cambridge University and his concern for the poor and the working class was borne out by the fact that he was also president of the Society for the Improvement of Conditions of the Labouring Classes, a group who he considered to shoulder most of the toil for little of the reward. I wonder if, deep down, he was a socialist rather than an imperialist at heart.

I'm sure you'd agree it is an impressive list of achievements, especially for a German who willingly made Great Britain his adopted home but who struggled for some time to be accepted by the establishment. Unfortunately, he died at only forty-two, leaving behind a bereft Queen Victoria and one to wonder what else he might have achieved in life had he lived on. I feel that as a human being he is entirely worthy of having a remote town, in a state that bears his wife's name, named in his honour. More worthy than others? Perhaps not, but then he was the husband of a queen, and not just of any queen, in an age when that meant everything.

Melbourne

'Tis a magical path
Of sensual curves suspended,
Topped by heralds unabashed.
To be ruined or mended.

From the setting sun
To the heart of the beast,
The wary traveller uncertain,
Whether famine or feast.

To the lair, to the lair,
Like moths to the flare,
On precious wings,
Be they burnt or fair.

A lady or a whore,
A giver or a taker,
A charmer or a terror,
A most liveable or a most lockable,
To breathe again
The life of the bay.
'Tis Melbourne.
Take her; she is yours.

It takes three hours for me to get to Melbourne via the Princes Freeway. I don't drive fast. I look after the old girl. I like Melbourne, in small packages, for it gives me things I cannot get where I live. When I go there, I generally stay at my sister's home with her boisterous schnauzer, ungrateful cat and aloof budgie.

I came to Melbourne for my sister's birthday. My niece, Natalie, and I celebrated Adrienne's birthday with pizza and wine in Yarraville followed by a movie, *Elvis*, at the Sun Theatre. It was a good night but yet again I found that my stomach can no longer tolerate too much pizza, or Elvis for that matter.

I set my departure for the fourth of July. I hoped to see my two children, Simon and Jessica, before I left but that wasn't possible. However, I did manage to have a good old boy's night out with a group of old and dear friends: Dave, Joe, John and Sisco. It seemed bizarre to them that I was doing such a trip, alone, for anything up to two months, for that was the estimate I had roughly come up with. It was a very rough estimate indeed, for I had no plan at all and nothing whatsoever had been booked. It was simply a case of hitting the road and see what happens; just the way I like it.

There seemed to be a pervading feeling amongst these resorts-are-the-only-way-to-have-a-real-holiday-type friends of mine that, journeying as I was, alone, into the wilds of Cape York, there was every chance that they might never see me again. I think they thought I was crazy. In the end, however, access to the cape was so much easier than I had anticipated and civilisation was so ubiquitous that I felt like a fraud and harboured a sensation that I had betrayed the opinion they revealed towards me as some sort of ballsy, if not suicidal, adventurer.

Day 1

The Newell,
Lordy, bless my soul, what a gruel!
For one of such fame
Could you not be more vain?
Or do you delight in making the fool.

Oh Newell,
Why be so cruel?
'Tis not cool
To have potholes the size of a pool
And crumbling edges be the rule.

Wretched Newell, 'tis not your fault,
That at the mention of your name the funds do bolt.
Your miserable tar
Is not worthy of a car
Unless it be sturdy of a jolt.

Dear Newell,
Fire powder and hurl tape,
For your infamy be finally bettered,
By a road, in name only, going to the Cape.

The fourth of July came quickly. I felt like I had everything I needed, nothing forgotten, nothing overlooked. Most importantly, my sister had given me a leather-bound journal in which, unlike what I would usually write on, it would be a pleasure to write, much like, I think, the difference between having wine out of a proper glass rather than a plastic cup.

But I digress into trivialities, which I am prone to do, I'm afraid to say. It is a tendency I will try to curtail for the sake of you, the reader, but there will be times when I shall fail, unfortunately, but at least I have had the decency to warn you. Still, the psychology of the analogy with the wine is very real; I am sure you agree. There is a real psychological pleasure in opening a leather-bound volume and penning some words. It is much more enticing and motivating than doing the same with scraps of paper or a cheap notebook.

It was late morning when I parted ways with Melbourne after a walk with my sister and her dog, a shower and a Facebook post. I decided to do the Facebook thing to keep my legion of friends informed, post photos and perhaps even amuse a few sods who have the luxury of some spare time to waste on my posts.

A sunny sky and the carefree feeling that comes with having nothing more complex to think about than following a trail of bitumen all day made me feel good to be alive. And it is good to be alive. I think that many of us so often forget that, so I will say it again: it is good to be alive.

It doesn't take much for me to be happy these days when I don't have the pressures of work, repayments and a family to raise. I do without unnecessary stuff, I don't need a great deal of money and, till now at least, I have been blessed with good health, which is something I work at and never take for granted. I have found, time and time again, through the years that I have thus far consumed, that it is the so-called small things that make life good and contribute most to a sense of happiness. I know it is a boring thing to say, I know that we have heard it all before, I know that it doesn't apply to everyone, but I strongly believe that it is a deep truth so I will say it again: small things make life good, doing good makes life good, kindness makes life good, being of good cheer makes life good.

The mostly flat and boring drive along the Hume, Goulburn Valley and Newell Highways was mostly detrimental to the sense of happiness which comes with an open road but it bothered me not, for I was on my way. Most of the country I had seen before and it is predominantly farms and irrigation. The highlights were a big strawberry and the world's biggest playable guitar but I stopped at neither, it being sufficient for me just to know that they exist somewhere in the vicinity. I cannot remember which towns they were in and I didn't write it down so if you really need to know, then Google it, and then I suggest you see a shrink.

For the first night of my trip, I camped on the north bank of the Murrumbidgee River on a scrappy piece of land to the side of a dirt road just downstream of Narrandera.

Dinner was very rudimentary, followed by a short stroll which happened to bring me to the final resting place of the PS *Wagga Wagga*, the last paddle-steamer to work on the Murrumbidgee. I couldn't see what is left of her but apparently some of the old girl is still visible when the river is low.

It is a melancholy place where she has ended up, after over forty years of faithful service on the river operating between Wagga and Hay, at the end of a forlorn and overgrown dirt track whose sole embellishments are potholes of various gauges and a variety of empty beer cans by the side, Great Northern being the most common species and, it seems to me, the bogan beer of choice nowadays. But at least there is a sign paying tribute to her and she now rests where she had for so long worked. She carried timber, wool, household goods, passengers and tourists and was apparently much loved. Perhaps she loved in return, in some way. Faithful service perhaps. But even the much-loved meet their end and for the PS *Wagga Wagga* the end came most remarkably on 11 November 1918! She hit a snag, holing her hull, and she was scuttled; I like to think at the eleventh hour. So ended a war and so ended the PS *Wagga Wagga*. (Reference: Australian Maritime Museum)

I woke to a frozen morning in the shade of river red gums with a beautiful blue sky beyond their canopy. As far as I was concerned, the only thing that remained unfrozen were the vocal cords of some neighbourly sulphur-crested cockatoos and the interminable revolutions of Kenworth engines on the Newell, a stone's throw away, passing through Narrandera.

There is something sublime about sitting on the bank of a river in the early morning mist, with the first cup of coffee, piping hot, watching the swirls of the water and the glint of sunlight coming from it. I simply sat and watched the Murrumbidgee. I kept watching as I sipped the coffee, in a contemplative mood, and then it came to me: what a beautiful name this river has. I kept saying Murrumbidgee to myself, out loud, over and over again, and in the process I decided that it must be the most beautiful name for a river in the whole country and perhaps even the world. It is such a delightful word to say. The United States has some great river names: the Shenandoah, Colorado and Mississippi come to mind. Maybe Shenandoah pips Murrumbidgee by a nose but it is a close-run thing.

My mind works in mysterious ways when I am idle, often baffling people, myself included. I drifted off thinking about other names, of places, and nearby Gundagai came to mind. It is another great name but, I thought, through no fault of its own, its name begins with gun, unfashionable, and a picture came to mind of a black-suited, white-tied mafioso telling some underling to 'gun-da-guy'. Stupid, I know. I beg your forgiveness as well as your understanding, for bizarre thoughts have plagued my life.

Day 2

The second day saw me continue my adventure northward, on the Newell; hardly a pleasure. It truly is a shit road. Recent flooding in NSW was evident with swollen rivers, flooded paddocks and one lane of the highway closed off at one point. Ominous clouds loomed to the north but for now I had sunshine.

I was as impressed by West Wyalong as I was unimpressed by the Newell. It has many old buildings and the town reminded me of Chiltern, in Victoria, but larger. To see drovers on horseback sidling up to its hotels and the horse and cart on its streets would seem more natural than the cars of nowadays but there you have it, times change, we move on. What seems romantic today was likely, in its day, to be anything but.

Somewhere around West Wyalong, I began once more to despair about the quality of my partner's sound system, but I have yet to do anything about it. The radio works, but it has a frustrating tendency for the volume to slip down when I am trying to turn it up. The cassette player has never worked; there is a length of wire shoved into the socket outside where the aerial should be that seems to do the trick, and it completely lacks anything more electronically advanced, that is to say, no CD player, no computer, no Bluetooth or any of that stuff.

That said, you could have the best car sound system money can buy but listening to country radio would still be shite. Too much trite talk, boring stuff, too many ads, and not enough music. The exception was an older man I managed to pick up on the radio a couple of times called Jack, who was actually entertaining and played damn good music but I couldn't tell you which radio station he hailed from because the display doesn't work. Anyway, he never seemed to last long before disappearing into a cloak of static, which was a shame. I missed Jack when he vanished for good.

A distressing sight befell me today around forty kilometres short of Dubbo. A large kangaroo was lying on the left shoulder of the highway, clearly unable to move but still alive with its head raised and moving. It was most upsetting. I stopped at a vet in Dubbo and the receptionist gave me the phone number for WIRES (Wildlife Information, Rescue, and Information Service). I rang them and a local volunteer was to be sent to deal with the stricken animal. These people are on call and do an incredible job, any time, day or night. They deserve our appreciation and respect for what they do.

For those who perhaps come from another solar system or are otherwise not in tune with this one, Dubbo is famous for its zoo but I gave it a miss. I was keen to get to sunny Queensland and besides, I had been there before during an ill-fated honeymoon road trip after marrying back in 1990. No doubt a lot of things have happened to the place since then but that was insufficient to entice me.

I had decided to stop for the night at Goobang National Park, well south of Dubbo, only to discover that the road to it was closed, presumably due to flooding, so, not for the last time, I found myself scratching around like a chook in leaf litter for somewhere to camp. It was getting late in the day and I felt my levels of frustration rising as every sidetrack led to private property and 'no camping' signs by the thousands seemed to pop out of the ground for their evening frolic and sadistic entertainment at the expense of the desperate and destitute traveller.

But, at least on this night, I hit the jackpot by taking the turn-off to the Gilgandra Flora Reserve just north of the town of Gilgandra. This little gem is six kilometres off the Newell, which meant a night free of traffic noise, and is a magnificent remnant of the native vegetation of the area complete with picnic shelter, barbecue, toilets, rubbish bins and a number of short walking tracks to explore the reserve. Needless to say, camping in the reserve is prohibited but no matter because, as I sleep in the tray of the Cruiser under a canvas canopy, all I need is a small cleared area of flattish land on which to park and move about a little and it was to be had just outside the entrance.

In case you haven't yet noticed, I am somewhat of a flora enthusiast and devout dendrophile so an after-dinner stroll to look at plants was definitely in order. Some plants I recognised, such as white and black cypress pines, mugga ironbark, various wattles, she-oak, heath, grass trees, Stypandra and Persoonia, but many others I wasn't familiar with, including Dwyer's redgum, two other species of ironbark, blue-leaved and narrow-leaved, and various shrubs and smaller plants. For me, as the evening light grew dim, it was a relaxing and satisfying way to end another day of gruel on the Newell.

That night, I thought of the kangaroo and I hoped that it was now at eternal rest. As I thought of that poor creature, a philosophical dilemma came to mind which I would like to put to you. Supposing, for the sake of discussion, that I had seen a wounded bull ant instead of a kangaroo by the side of the road. What to do and why? Should I call WIRES? Clearly not. I can imagine the reaction of the WIRES person. But then I found myself asking myself; why not? Is not a bull ant's life just the same as a kangaroo's life as far as the universe is concerned, or, if you believe in such things, were they not both created by the same deity, as equals, without preference for one or the other and provided space, again as equals, on Noah's ark?

It is humans who judge the relative value of lives. We see them differently, as having lives of unequal value. In making such a judgement, it is clear that size and numbers matter. We value larger animals more, especially mammals; understandably so, for we are large mammals. We identify with mammals, they are more like us, and besides, who cares about a single bull ant when there are trillions of the little critters everywhere?

I wondered at what creature along the spectrum do we draw the line? It is a ridiculous and pointless thought but the sort of thing that comes to me during long evenings alone, when couples would engage in sex but there is little else for me to do than think and read. I wondered too if this is in some way the fundamental root of racism: the intrinsic placing of greater value on those who are more like us; an instinct born of fear or a common culture, and/or a sense of superiority born of ignorance and suspicion and an innate belief that our way must be best.

As if the musings above had not burdened my mind enough, I had a nightmare about the Newell that night. I was driving and it was getting late and I was looking for a turn-off where I could camp when a wide-load escort vehicle drove past me, with its amber lights flashing, but it also had searchlights that shone into the cabin of my car, blinding me. I heard the roar of the prime mover that was pulling the wide load getting louder and louder in a terrifying crescendo, but I couldn't see it. Once the escort vehicle passed and my eyesight recovered, I saw it at the very last moment and I swerved to miss the wide load of whatever it was, a huge black metallic structure, but as I swerved the load got wider and the more I swerved the wider it got, so there was no way of avoiding it. Finally, it crashed through my windscreen but I don't know what came after that. I didn't wake, but it was pretty scary stuff and I hoped that it would not be an omen for the day's resumption with the challenges the Newell presents to the person behind the wheel: derelict narrow road, big trucks, and I have never seen so many wide loads in my life.

At the risk of being trite, I want to harp on about the Newell a bit more. It is so bad that it needs to be said. I had heard talk about it in the past from grey nomads and others but I thought it was just more of their bitching and whingeing, you know how it goes, never-satisfied types complete with exaggeration just to make a good yarn, first-world problems, et cetera; so I paid them scant attention as their complaints hammered away at my switched-off mind and seized-up ossicles, from where they languorously drifted away.

The Newell is something you must experience for yourself to fully appreciate its deplorable state. For a major back door link between Victoria, New South Wales and southern Queensland, that must carry thousands of heavy trucks every day, its condition is unfathomable. Single lane for most of its length, frequent potholes, crumbling surface and edges with loose stones waiting patiently to become destructive projectiles; fortunate indeed is the windscreen which manages to survive any significant part of the highway's length undamaged or intact. My windscreen had no such fortune; it sustained two new cracks and a number of scratches, while the paintwork at the front end of the car became peppered with chips.

Somebody, do something about it! Please! It seems that they are, in a way, judging by the fact that there were roadworks every five minutes, but it doesn't seem to make any difference!

Having had my say on the Newell, I will now forever hold my peace; maybe.

Day 3

The morning of the third day was cold, grey and wet. I did another walk around the reserve and then there was nothing for it but to push on to Queensland with the hope of better weather.

I drove all day through much cotton country, the white balls of cotton lining the edges of the road, reminiscent of snow, being the giveaway. I went through Coonabarabran, avoiding the lure of the Warrumbungles, which I had visited before, through Narrabri, avoiding the lure of Mt Kaputar, which I had visited before, Moree, Bogabilla, which is a dive, Goondiwindi, which looks OK, and shortly after I said goodbye and good riddance to the Newell as I picked up the Barwon heading to St George. This is a much better highway and the traffic is far lighter. Often, I had long stretches of empty road before me which gladdened the soul and did wonders for the spirit. Freedom; hassle-free freedom.

I stopped for the night in a small town called Bungunya. With the weather having improved considerably, even this place failed to pour water on my mood; initially.

Once upon a time, Bungunya would have been known as a shabby one-horse town but nowadays it has progressed magnificently to a shabby two-ute town; the rolling ground of noble hard cars with rusted bodies, with pumps and other useful stuff in the back, and driven by hard, no-nonsense men wearing cowboy hats. The unnerving effect is completed by a smattering of dead-looking houses, desolate-looking grain silos and a desultory-looking railway line coming from God knows where and going to the same place. I can sum up the appearance of the town in one word: disused. No, make that two words: disused and creepy.

I felt like a foreigner and, just like a foreigner, I became a little paranoid. I felt observed, and that made me somewhat jittery. I stopped for the night at a small reserve with a picnic shelter and a couple of rubbish bins and with the drab public toilet block nearby. I was alone and I felt vulnerable in this hick-looking joint.

In my semi-paranoid state, which wasn't improved when a dusty dark-blue Falcon with a spoiler, rumbling exhaust and tinted windows drifted past, I didn't want any of the locals to get the wrong idea about a solitary male parked just outside the dunnies. With hindsight, I can chuckle to myself about it now because the locals probably didn't give a damn whether I was there or not. To them, I would have been just another blow-in stopping for the night, I'm sure; giving nothing, taking nothing; but at the time, the thoughts were real and I was only half joking with my paranoid self as I imagined deviant eyes locked onto me from the handful of cars slowly rolling through town like roulette balls about to come to a stop on the wheel, on my number.

After dinner, I did my usual dental routine but I flossed as inconspicuously as possible. Trying my best to fit in, I thought that one of the hard men of the town might take exception to a flossing blow-in pansy parked outside the toilets giving his town a bad reputation and as a result, after as much due process as a mind like that can process, make his lumbering way towards me and proceed to redesign my dentition in such a way as to make future flossing unnecessary.

Needless to say, I retired to my cocoon early that night and there I stayed until I took flight early next morning as soon as the kookaburras called. A lonely train came through in the night. It seemed to intensify my sense of desolation. Another came by next morning, going the other way as I was preparing to leave, and a cherry-picker drove slowly up the main road as if looking for something to do.

The night was not entirely without drama. At some point, what sounded like a large truck parked nearby. It sounded like it would park on top of me. I heard the truckie go to the toilet and visions of Spielberg's *Duel* came to me, raising my paranoia to incandescent levels. The truck left shortly after and only then could I allow myself the luxury of going back to a fitful sleep.

I have one final comment to make about Bungunya and then it will be filed away with the Newell and I will forever hold my peace on it as well. It concerns street names. The main street is called Main Street – fair enough, it makes perfect sense in a sensible town to have a name like that for its main street and I cannot raise any objection to it whatsoever even in my smart-arse frame of mind – but I couldn't help noticing as I drove along Main Street to leave town for good, another street going off to the left by the name of Beach Street. Now, that seemed odd. I may be wrong and forgive me if, in my ignorance, I am mistaken, but such a name in such a town can only be the result of extreme optimism or extreme delusion. There is a third possibility, though unlikely, and that is that it is an extremely long street, particularly given that it heads in a westerly direction!

Day 4

Anyway, not my problem; onward I drive, leaving Bungunya to disappear from my rear-view mirror for good and hoping to get close to Carnarvon Gorge today.

The next proper town I went through was St George, which is slap-bang in the middle of cotton country, then came Surat and somewhere between the two was a sign that declared, perhaps with some official pomp behind it, that you were entering the Queensland Outback.

I could not help thinking, perhaps with a twist of melodrama tossed in, that it is now fair dinkum; the time has come to face the demons and the serious business begins; from now on, if you run out of water, fuel or your car (or mind for that matter) has a breakdown out this way, you die. But I was naïve in thinking that way, you see, for I had no idea what I was really in for. The image I had of the never-never, where the price of a mishap is death, was somewhat tempered by the fact that there were caravans, camper-trailers, and four-wheel drives everywhere; that, and also the fact of having the good fortune to score a couple of free hotdogs and a hot coffee in Surat, a town at the very frontier of the Queensland outback. It was comforting but also a bit of a disappointment as, in no time at all, I had gone from a fearless adventurer, albeit one who flosses, to merely being one of the crowd where the greatest danger was from overeating fast food or being trampled in the rush for cheap fuel at the next servo. So much for outback danger and deprivations. I felt a tad let down.

The free tucker came courtesy of NAIDOC week or, more precisely, the ratepayers of whichever shire Surat finds itself in. The very pleasant woman who gave me the food and coffee might have thought I needed fattening up; in any case, they were the last two hot dogs and there seemed to be no other takers, the festivities beginning to wind down, and the smattering of people who remained were half asleep and mostly quite rotund and already well satisfied in the gastrointestinal department I'm sure.

She told me that the shire had funded the spread as well as the live entertainment in celebration of NAIDOC week. The muso was just as good as the hot dogs with fried onion. Both went down very well. I didn't catch the muso's name but he had a good voice, a bit gravelly, which reminded me of Joe Cocker. He played the guitar well too. I'm not really a fan of most country music and once the guitars start wailing, I go insane but his own take on country music was good and his songs told a tale. He also performed some hits of Creedence, Michael Jackson and others. It really was a most pleasant hour spent in glorious sunshine, warmth and a picturesque park. When it was over, I left somewhat unwillingly but with a full belly and raised spirits.

Surat stood out for me for another reason too: the first time I had seen bottle trees *(Brachychiton rupestris)* in the flesh. Boring, I hear you say, but I was amazed by them. I am very familiar with their relative, found in Victoria, known as the kurrajong *(Brachychiton populneus)*, which I have grown from seed and whose seeds were once roasted and used as a coffee substitute; a rather poor one, I would imagine. Anyway, irrelevant; it was great seeing them.

The first real drama of the trip occurred in Roma, where I stopped to do some food shopping and managed to lock the keys in the car; by no means for the first time. Fortunately, the mishap was easily rectified as the driver's side window was down sufficiently for me to reach the little doover on the door which locks it, with a wire cheerfully provided by the local Toyota dealer, the pub I was parked near having been unable to help despite my offer to buy a six-pack if they could find some suitable wire. So my bacon was saved, but not before I had to traipse back to the Toyota dealer to get a bevel cut on the end of the wire so it would dig in and grip the plastic doover on the door to lift it up.

Roma is a big place so I didn't hang about once all the chores were done. Of more interest to me, having an Italian background, is how Roma got its name. If anyone can tell me, please let me know.

After the delay caused by having to break into my car, it was clear that I wasn't going to reach Carnarvon Gorge before dark and, as I am very reluctant to drive in the evening or at night due to the higher risk of hitting wildlife, I was forced to stop elsewhere for the night.

I tried to find Expedition National Park but I must have turned off too soon and, after crossing a couple of streams, I somehow ended up in a scrappy bit of bush that looked nothing like a national park, about thirteen kilometres from the main road. But it was quiet and it served its main purpose, which was simply to provide a place to sleep, satisfactorily.

A particularly cold night and a crispness around the ears told me that once I stuck my head out of the canvas I would be greeted by clear skies and that was indeed the case.

Day 5

I couldn't wait to get to Carnarvon; to finally see what for so long I had merely heard about and also, after so long spent sitting at the wheel, doing some decent walks.

What can I say about Carnarvon Gorge? Mere words can scarcely do it justice and even photos fall a long way short of representing its soaring grandeur and amazing detail. For me, Carnarvon Gorge is a place of sublime beauty and a place where natural miracles really do happen.

> Carnarvon Gorge is a place
> Where blue is bluer
> And green is greener
> And you feel a lightyear from cares.

I arrived at ten in the morning and the car park was already almost overflowing. It was school holidays and there were people everywhere. The campground was full so I would have to find a place outside the park to spend the two nights I planned to stay. But none of that seemed to matter somehow. I was there, the sun was shining, it was warm, people were happy and almost without fail greeted you on the track. It was simply a great place to be and I think everyone else felt the same way.

I couldn't get walking fast enough. My body yearned to move. I immediately did the 1.5-kilometre nature walk as an entrée but I was a little disappointed to find that none of the plants were labelled. As a stranger to the area, I was most curious to know what I was looking at. That's the problem with a lot of so-called nature walks: they invariably have either no signs at all or a few simplistic, dumbed-down signs that are next to useless to anyone with anything more than the most rudimentary interest in the natural world.

Not to worry, though; having got that small gripe off my chest, nature can be appreciated without the signs, and any disappointment I felt was swept aside by the fan palms, river she-oaks, sedges and reeds along the bank of Carnarvon Creek and, higher up, the cycads, some with two-metre trunks, wattles in flower, Exocarpos, Hardenbergia, ironbarks, spotted gums and a curious eucalypt I hadn't seen before with tessellated bark at the lower end of the trunk which I was later to find out is *Corymbia tessellaris*. It is a most impressive tree chiefly for its curious bark.

Then I stopped and stared in wonder at a pair of platypuses frolicking in a clear, tranquil pool of the creek, as if fully appreciative of the joy of life and dancing to its serendipitous tune.

The next walk I did was to Boolimba Bluff, a 6.4-kilometre return trip with some very steep sections requiring rock steps, steel ladders and some heavy breathing. It was a slog but I felt all the better for it. From the top of the bluff, I was hoping for good views up the gorge but I had to settle for impressive views to the south overlooking the visitor centre and east over flat plains to distant mountains.

Having warmed up and given the legs a good workout, there was no stopping me now. On to the Rockpool next, where I sat in the sun for some time; resting, thinking and watching. There were birds, a turtle in the pool and some young people who went for a swim in the chilled water. Of course I thought about it, as the pool looked so inviting. Forty years ago, I would have been in like Flynn, just try and stop me; thirty years ago, there might or might not have been some qualms, but given short shrift; twenty years ago, I would have done it with some discomfort but without hesitation to impress the kids; ten years ago, I would have done it with added discomfort and some hesitation, if I was with friends, to prove that I still had what it takes and to polish the tarnish from my mettle. These days, forget it. I feel the cold a lot more and yet, paradoxically, I prefer a cooler climate to a warmer one. 'Tis one of the oddities that go with ageing, I suppose. It would take a much hotter day or a significant cash dare to tempt me to cloak myself in the water's chilled cloth and neither presented themselves on this day.

I should elaborate; the Rockpool is a beautiful pool in Carnarvon Creek about 200 metres from the car park, which is a two-kilometre drive from the visitor centre. I was happy to bask by its edge and immerse myself merely in contemplation and to write in my journal. I left the watery frolicking to the young 'uns.

I finished the day with the three-kilometre return walk to Mickey Creek Gorge. A gentle amble along this track was the perfect way to spend the evening. It was too nice to walk fast and my weary legs wouldn't allow it anyway. There were tall palms, cycads with four-metre tall trunks, a trickle coming from the creek, and high cliffs that blocked out the setting sun, adding a coolness to the air.

It is odd, I thought, the little things that sometimes stay with you, that seem to be burnished into one's memory forever, often for no particular reason. Seemingly not always the greatest or the most beautiful, but for some reason such snippets are snatched from obscurity, implanted and cannot be forgotten.

Coming from Victoria, seeing elkhorn ferns in the wild was new to me and there was one specimen growing on a rock right at the end of the track. There was nothing special about it; it didn't speak to me, it didn't dance, I'd seen plenty of others that day, but I guess it was in the right place at just the right time and I still remember it vividly. It seemed special somehow, just as the day had been special.

Day 6

The following day, I awoke with grand plans; to walk up the gorge to Cathedral Cave and back, an 18.2-kilometre return trip. But all that was soon derailed by my weakness in the face of temptation and, yes, I'm afraid that I am vulnerable to temptation. I confess to enjoying a whisky or two now and then. More rarely, I will puff on a cigar with great delight but too much will make my head spin and fill me with nausea. Similarly, the correct dose of pleasant female company now and then is a fillip, but for me, the greatest temptations are the wonders of the natural world.

To walk along a bush track, seeing where it takes me, is a compulsion. To have a bush track in my vicinity and not walk along it and thereby miss out on its unknown wonders is an agony I can barely endure. So I promptly gave in to each and every little fascinating side trip that I came upon, with the inevitable result that I ran out of time and energy to get to Cathedral Cave. It is not my fault that I failed to achieve my objective; I blame my subconscious mind. It is too easily tempted. It wanders down lanes and sidings. It has the devil in it. Dionysus shacks up in it from time to time and creates havoc. You cannot win. It is never satisfied.

I snatched each little prize along the way and by doing so missed out on the grand one. I saw absolute marvels but I will never know what I missed out on seeing and that torments me. Easy? Life is not meant to be. Not to worry. You cannot have everything, I told myself as a feeble comfort. Let them eat cake, but then you cannot have them. Temptation is a bugger to resist.

Once more, the sun was shining, the sky was blue, I was walking up the gorge, and the legs were feeling fine after yesterday's exertions. It felt good to be alive and to have a day full of glories ahead. There were many other walkers out that day, many families with children, and I could tell that most of them felt the same way as I did; well, perhaps not the children, but people were happy, carefree, relaxed. Mortgages, school fees and tax bills were shoved in a dark corner of the cerebral attic. They looked at you and smiled or said g'day. I felt the absence of the outrage that seems so pervasive nowadays. We were all under the spell of the place.

My head kept turning one way and the other, spying vegetation, cliffs, and the creek, always the creek, winding its way through the gorge and the numerous crossings of it, all of them of the rock-hopping type instead of on the fancy footbridges that mostly predominate, as it should be, how it is meant to be.

I got to a place called the Art Gallery having, with enormous difficulty, walked straight past sidetracks to places with enticing names like the Moss Garden, the Amphitheatre and Ward's Canyon, admittedly with an unmistakeable slowing of the steps that accompanied the simultaneous formation of two minds.

The Art Gallery was sublime: the best example of Aboriginal rock art I had ever seen. The artists used white ochre (kaolin) and red ochre (haematite) to create sprayed handprints, boomerang prints, goannas and numerous white or red criss-cross patterns, each indicating the burial of someone nearby. There are also carvings of emu eggs in the rock walls as well as innumerable carvings of female genitalia taking up a large area of the rock space. Each is approximately life-size and there must be hundreds of the things. The explanatory sign did the polite thing and duly explained them as being something vaguely to do with fertility but I can't help wondering if a whole lot of young males couldn't help themselves and created them while laughing and giggling amongst themselves. I suspect that boys will be boys whatever the culture and however long ago it might be.

Unfortunately, the place had been vandalised in the past by idiots adding their own graffiti to it. One is even dated, 1952. Idiots abound, I'm afraid, and one of their characteristics is to seek out and destroy anything of value to others. They respect nothing.

I had lunch and a drink. I looked at the art and then I looked at it again. Then I had to make a decision: to push on to Cathedral Cave or return and take in all the side trips. Not for the first or last time, I had to tell myself that I couldn't do everything, which is an attitude that goes against my grain. Finally, lured by the wonderful-sounding destinations, I decided to turn back and see them all.

The first port of call was Ward's Canyon, where a track leads up beside a small waterfall into a narrow, shaded canyon above, which contains remnant rainforest. This tiny area is remarkable, a living fossil, containing very tall tree ferns (around ten metres tall) and is the only inland site in Queensland where the beautiful king fern is to be found, with its short trunk giving rise to remarkable fronds that are five to six metres long! There they have survived, protected from harm in the cool, moist and shady canyon, embraced by steep rocky cliffs. There are not many, they are incredibly special, and it was a privilege to see them.

However, good as Ward's Canyon was, it was the Amphitheatre which really blew me away and was for me the highlight of the day. A metal stepladder takes you up to an opening in the rock cliff above, like a narrow crevice, through which you enter a passage. I pictured the scene from *Picnic at Hanging Rock* where the girls magically disappear into the rocks, to vanish. I thought of the film's haunting music. As I walked along the passage, I thought of what wonders I would behold at the end of it.

A small stream exits from the crevice and drops away. You follow the creek along the passage for a short way before it opens into a huge rock chamber, just like an amphitheatre, with a crevice at the opposite end from which the stream enters. One can picture the creek in flood, becoming a watery juggernaut carving out the inside of the rock and, over thousands of years, creating the chamber it is today. The roof is a cupola of rock with a small aperture, like a skylight, through which one can see some trees and a patch of sky. The floor is mostly rock and ferns. I was stunned for a while. I sat on one of the benches and pondered the incredible constructions of nature. I created echoes. I took photos and a video, but they in no way captured the enormousness of what I was experiencing.

The final side-trip was to the Moss Garden. Again, it is a remarkable feat of nature: a garden of mosses, lichens and liverworts kept constantly moist regardless of the season through the combined efforts of rain, gravity and the interplay of rock of differing porosity.

Rain falls onto the sandstone high above, beyond the clifftops, and it slowly percolates through the massive layer of sandstone, hundreds of metres thick, until, at the bottom end, it strikes impervious shale and is forced to emerge from the cliff between the two layers of rock to trickle onto the moss gardens below, thereby keeping the garden constantly moist. It is quite an accomplishment of natural hydrology. Also extraordinary is the fact that the emerging water fell as rain hundreds of years ago and has taken that long to percolate through the sandstone. We may be in a hurry, we may be impatient, but nature never is.

It was a wonderful day and I mean that in the true sense of the word; it was full of wonders. But like all days, good and bad, it ended. Back at my camp, a good Samaritan pulled up and told me that I was still within the national park boundary and risked a fine. My mistake. I thought I was outside the park. Anyway, I didn't want a fine, surprise surprise, so I moved, searching in vain for a place to stop until I got to Rolleston, only to find that camping is prohibited at the town's reserve.

This was annoying but soon rectified as I found a large, open, wayside stop just out of town where the Carnarvon and Dawson highways meet.

My sleep was interrupted by a couple of big trucks that shared the place with me; both arriving late, leaving early and making a great deal of noise in the process. Still, where would we be without trucks? In a very different place.

Day 7

A freezing night and a bitey morning once more heralded a sunny day; perfection where yesterday had been beautiful. I took the Dawson to Springsure where, a short distance out of the town and still on the Dawson, I discovered a gem: Minerva Hills National Park.

Oddly enough, it is named after a Roman goddess who, having just had a quick look at her credentials, was the goddess for just about everything that is good and virtuous including wisdom, justice, arts, sciences, medicine, family, bravery et cetera. The list goes on. Quite a woman. Faultless. Perfection. A delight to have at any dinner party, I'm sure, at least until her goodness ruined it for everyone else and her omniscience became a tedious bore. I am not at all acquainted with her character, whether considerate or condescending.

Like all know-alls and the ultra-good, she may have ridden a high horse which she rarely, if ever, dismounted, romped the high ground, and stacked soapboxes one on top of another, using her omniscience as a weapon of power and a tool for condescension or, perhaps, as part of her general goodness, she may have shown restraint and given other opinions a go only to, naturally, modestly trump them in the end with the final authoritative word. I really have no idea and I do not give a fig one way or the other, except as a minor curiosity, because I care not for gods and goddesses.

But I jest, because even though the good can be boring if they are too good, there is not enough goodness in the world, and I cannot help liking her, as she is associated with the owl (which is perhaps why the owl is associated with wisdom), the olive tree and the hellebore plant.

Her old man was Jupiter and, according to Wikipedia, her old girl was Metis, an Oceanid nymph, whatever that means.

Enough of ancient Roman goddesses and back to the national park which bears her name for it is well worth the small detour to visit it and for reasons which have nothing to do with ancient Rome – although it does add further evidence supporting my theory that Australia was once invaded by Roman legions – and more to do with natural beauty and spectacular views.

A rough road rises from the west, makes its way past forests, rocky terrain and low scrub plateaus to reach the escarpment to the east from which rocky peaks dramatically arise. There are several lookouts from where it is possible to see Springsure and the valleys below but none better than the Skyline Lookouts, a short walk from the final car park. The view to Mt Zamia, named after the genus of cycads, and its Virgin Rock is astounding. An image of Mary and Jesus is meant to be visible from the town side of the rock and is highlighted at night but unfortunately I wasn't there at the right time to see it.

Stop for a rest or a picnic at Fred's Gorge picnic area, a very pretty spot with tall trees, a creek running nearby, and a great view downstream to the falls and a gorge far below. It is made all the better by irresponsible and dangerous rock-hopping, which I am totally against and would not recommend to anyone, to a much better vantage point at the top of the falls from which one can see the water plunge down.

To do it, one has to skirt around a wire fence, which is easy enough as all one has to do is walk to the end of the fence a few metres away, and the rock-hopping that I allegedly did was easy. Surprisingly, and much to my delight, there is no barrier at the top of the falls, a rarity these days; and, even more surprising and rarer still, was the complete absence of warning signs that generally detract from the experience of a oneness with nature. I suspect that we have the legal profession to thank for the plethora of idiotic signs and barriers that one sees everywhere nowadays. Human beings must be pretty dumb if they must be warned of every conceivable little common-sense danger rather than take responsibility for it themselves. It seems that it never fails to be others who must be held to account.

After Minerva, I took the Gregory to Emerald, where I found diesel at a cheapish price. After refuelling, I made as quick an exit as it was possible to make while sticking to the speed limit. Where my distorted mind had for some inexplicable reason pictured gems and greenness in a town that goes by the name of Emerald, in reality, I had merely stumbled upon another large town with people, traffic, traffic lights and Harvey Norman.

Approaching Emerald, a large sign proclaimed it to be 'The Heart of the Central Highlands'. I took exception to that on two grounds. First, being familiar with much of the mountainous country of Victoria, New South Wales and Tasmania, it seemed rather odd to me for the region to be given the highlands moniker. Most of the country looked low to me, albeit peppered with hills, low mountains and rugged escarpments. It is all relative, I suppose, and perhaps my judgement was askew. Second, I think if the heart is to be found anywhere, it would be beating in Carnarvon Gorge and not in a nondescript town with thousands of people, suburbia, traffic, traffic lights and 'Aich En'. I would more likely refer to Emerald as the rectum of the central highlands rather than its heart but that's just my opinion.

So, with that off my chest, I continued along the Great Inland Way. I'm not sure where I picked the great way up or, for that matter, where it starts and where it finishes, but I have been on it for some time now and it is taking me in the right direction, so I'll stick with it. It took me into the tropics, just north of Emerald, then on to Capella, where I considered having a blessed hot shower for free at the public toilets but decided against it as my stuff was too disorganised to get at. I don't shower too often. Bad for the skin. Removes the protective layer of paste formed by natural oils mixed with grime. Laziness. Tedious. Waste of time.

Next stop was Clermont, where I walked around Hoods Lagoon and was confronted by an odd site, a piano in a tree no less. This monument to the destructive 1916 flood, which claimed sixty-five lives, is a replica of one of three pianos found in trees once the water receded.

The walk around the lagoon is most pleasant with lots of birds and a fragrant plantation of lemon-scented gum adjacent. It gets the thumbs-up from me.

You definitely get a taste of the outback between Clermont and Belyando Crossing. The country is flat, the red earth is redder, the vegetation is more sparse and scrappy, the scattered farm dams look more vital and death is more apparent and even seems to be part of the essence. Dead plants and animals abound and are less distressing now and the bleached bones and desiccated carcasses that line the roadside seem to belong. The sole luxury is the bitumen.

My intention was to stop for the night at Mazeppa National Park but somehow I missed it. Either the signage is very obscure or it no longer exists. I did see a sign to Mazeppa quarry, so maybe there was a bob or two to be made so they dug the park up. I jest; a quick Google confirmed that the park is still in existence and also informed me that its name is derived from a character in a poem by Byron.

It seems extraordinary that a reference to a work by Byron should find itself out here, in the middle of nowhere, amongst featureless plains for, whatever you may think of Byron's lifestyle, he was certainly neither featureless nor plain. Hardly flattering to Byron who, I'm sure, would have been less than impressed and yet, for one described by an ex-wife as mad, bad and dangerous to know, if that is to be believed, it is perhaps no more than he deserves; but for his poetry.

I was more successful in locating Blackwood National Park, further north, although the sign is easily missed. The gate was locked, allowing entry only to walkers or cyclists, so I camped in the car park. I had the place to myself and some currawongs, courting for a feed, no doubt. They moved on when nothing was forthcoming.

What I could see of the park was not inspiring but I went for an after-dinner stroll nonetheless. It appears that there is a perimeter track which I took first in a clockwise direction, going for about half a kilometre until I reached a creek and surrounding swamps that forced me to turn back. The bush is scrubby woodland. Going anticlockwise was much the same. Nothing much seemed to be in flower. I turned back after a kilometre or so as it was getting late, with a feeling of bemusement. I am not sure about some of these national parks in Queensland. Unless I am missing something out of ignorance, I am not sure how this place qualifies as a park of national significance other than it perhaps being a rare remnant of what was once widespread. I found the place disappointing, not that I saw much of it.

Day 8

Day eight was rather boring. One of the highlights was experiencing the immense pleasure of driving on red bitumen; different at least. I'm all for it. Why stop there? Why not other colours? Two-tone roads perhaps; rainbows? It's worth bringing up at least. Make roads more interesting, a highlight in themselves, full of colours and wonders like in Mario Kart. It might stop people falling asleep as they do on uninspiring grey bitumen.

Then there were the long stretches of pink flowers, weeds, I suspect, but impressive nonetheless, on either side of the highway acting like pink runners. They were a cheerful sight and worthy of note, to my mind at least.

That's how dull the day was – when the colour of the bitumen and roadside weeds were the highlights. It was enough to make my mind drift once more into the realm of strange thought. I was thinking, today, as I drove along, that I have now become one of the grey nomads. One of those from down south who, like migrating birds, head north for the winter in search of destinations that have warmth in common.

It disturbs me a little, not because of the name, for there can be no denying my greyness nor a nomadic tendency, but because of the implication that I am joining a throng, all doing the same thing, like sheep. This is entirely disagreeable to one who considers himself to be a non-conformist and who has tried many moulds through a buckled span of life and never quite fitted entirely into any of them. Perhaps I am not as non-conformist as I like to think, and yet people have always been surprised whenever I have told them what I did for a crust, and now, here I am, having given up a good earner and chosen instead to go down the poverty-strewn path of plant propagating and writing. Lord help me, does that make me qualified as a non-conformist or merely a fool? I do not know. I am what I am, but if being part of a grey horde is what it takes to discover this wonderful land in one's grey years, then so be it. I have no choice. I neither wish to beat them nor join them; I simply want to do my own thing.

There was nothing dull about Charters Towers; not the part that I saw anyway, excluding the supermarket of course. She is a grand old dame and a grand old gold town with some stunning architecture. It is a place where grand old unkempt men with long beards and who love a drink say g'day to you in the street.

It is also where I did a little food shopping in a not so grand and not so old supermarket. I really do hate the places but, I'm ashamed to say, my bush tucker skills are definitely sub-par and I, along with just about everyone else, would perish without them.

While at the checkout queue, feeling lame in body and soul, feeling like a eunuch, a woman with an overflowing trolley let me go ahead of her. This random act of kindness was most appreciated so I sneakily bought her a Kit-Kat and gave it to her just as I was about to leave. I love doing that: a random act rewarded by another random act. In a world too full of anger and sadness, the surprised smiles of joy and appreciation delight me. I have done it before and it is well worth a dollar or two just to see the reaction you get from people. I hope it cheers them as much as it cheers me.

I was on the prowl for an op shop too, specifically one that sold second-hand books. I seek them out like stains seek a white shirt, particularly as I'd finished the book I was reading, Helen Garner's *This House of Grief*, so I was in desperate need of something else to read. I found the right place where I immediately hit the jackpot, finding *Vanity Fair* by William Makepeace Thackeray and *A Brief History of Time* by Stephen Hawking, for a few dollars. I knew I'd struck a seam and I felt like bringing the ghostly cries of eureka in this old gold town back to life.

So it wasn't such a bad day after all. I planned to stop for the night at the Lynd Roadhouse but, in the mistaken belief that it was on the road I was on, I drove straight past the turn-off and I hate turning back to anything. Not to worry. I stopped at a roadside clearing a bit further on. Just like my car, my gear and my set-up, it was nothing flash but it would do.

I had now entered tropical North Queensland. A sign somewhere south of the Lynd told me so. That evening, with the cape looming, I decided that the next time I had mobile coverage I should do some research on the roads and river crossings there as I had done bugger-all so far. I was worried about crossing the Wenlock and Jardine Rivers alone, and without a snorkel. What a dope! That's how totally ignorant I was. I didn't realise at the time that a bridge now crosses the Wenlock and a ferry crosses the Jardine!

Day 9

> The Crooked River flows
> Where no man ever goes.
> To a place where honest trees grow hollows,
> Their roots sup the cherished earth,
> Their boughs kiss the sacred air,
> Untainted by greed's foul breath.
> Taking only what is needed in admirable measure.
> A place where all is fair.

I digressed into poetry. Some days ago, I can't remember where, I had crossed a small river by the name of Crooked and it stuck with me.

The day was warm and humid, with clouds of the white fluffy kind. It would be a day of contrasts, beginning in outback-type country, going on to volcanic craters, before ending in tropical rainforest.

I made straight for Undara National Park to see the famous lava tubes, a side trip which turned out to be both fascinating and frustrating.

The fascinating bit was the walk around Kalkani crater. It is unmistakeable as a crater, although the views down into it are obscured by quite thick vegetation. The explanatory signage is good and adds to the delightful experience of ambling along its rim. I'm sure that you will no longer be surprised to know that the plants growing along the perimeter held the most interest for me; ones I'd never seen before thriving in such an unusual habitat, amongst the rugged basalt rocks, known as semi-evergreen vine thicket, a type of dry rainforest much more prevalent in the past. Here it survives, protected from fires by the rocks. The most notable plant, I think, is the bat's wing coral tree (*Erythrina vespertilio*). This native tree is unusual in that it is deciduous and the spectacular scarlet, bell-shaped flowers emerge on naked branches, before the branches are clothed in leaves. I was lucky enough to see some flowers in bloom.

The Kalkani volcano is a scoria cone, formed when the magma is combined with gases to explode and produce the aerated stone, known as scoria, on cooling. It erupted 190 to 400 thousand years ago. The last eruption in the area was a mere twenty thousand years ago. There may be more in the future but I wasn't too concerned for my safety.

Looking towards the east from the rim, one can see the Undara volcano, which erupted around 190,000 years ago. Radiating from its cone are lines of greener vegetation indicative of increased levels of moisture associated with the lava tubes.

The tubes are the longest in Australia and the longest from a single volcano of recent origin in the world. They began as flowing lava, along watercourses and depressions in the terrain, then, as the surface of the lava cooled and hardened while the deeper lava remained hot and continued to flow, the tubes were created, forming elongated caves that one can walk along.

I wanted to see one close-up, naturally enough, but it is only possible as part of a guided tour and I hate those things. I like to do my own thing in my own time and not be shepherded around like a sheep in a flock. I didn't want to hang around for the next one to start anyway and, if you'll pardon my cynicism, having to pay someone to show you around your own country is anathema to me and I couldn't help smelling the unpleasant odour of a money-making racket.

So, having seen some fascinating things, I left with an unwelcome feeling of disappointment and a bad taste. Never mind; plenty of other great places await the traveller who has no plan.

What awaited me were waterfalls, history, some of the most beautiful rainforest imaginable and a cold beer, all at or near the pretty town of Ravenshoe.

I'm not a big drinker but nor am I averse to the occasional glass or two and sometimes, if circumstance demands it, more. I'll drink anything that appeals to me at the time or pretty much anything that's on offer. Beer if the weather's hot, wine with food, whisky the rest of the time. Fortifieds, spirits, liqueurs, and cocktails when I can get them. Do not tell anyone this but alcohol is great. It tastes good and makes you feel good and opens a world of fun because people begin to relax and talk more and do strange things. Having said that, please drink responsibly because I need a lawsuit as much as I need a bowel obstruction.

The point is that, of course, I had to have a beer at the bar of the highest pub in Queensland, the Ravenshoe Hotel. With a claim to fame like that, the Ravenshoe must do very well, as any tourist who isn't a teetotaller would do exactly the same thing as I did.

Anyway, I have jumped ahead of myself in the excitement of having a beer at the highest pub. Before Ravenshoe, I stopped at Millstream Falls, the first of many falls I would see on this trip, until a detour to yet another waterfall would finally no longer appeal. Yes, let me break this to you gently: it is possible to get sick of waterfalls, I'll vouch for that.

The falls were impressive; plenty of water cascading over a ledge with a good roar and a good fall. Just as interesting was the site of an old World War II Australian army camp. There is a one-kilometre circuit track around the site and from it one can see many relics and the imagination goes to work filling in the rest. There is part of the original rock-lined walking track, old corduroyed roads, drains, concrete slabs, a flagpole site, a parade ground site which is still evident from the reduced amount of vegetation, and several partially caved-in trenches which were used for training purposes.

Many such camps were set up around Atherton for military training in jungle environments. The Millstream site is the best preserved and catered for around a thousand personnel. It was easy to imagine machine gunners going to work from the trenches and mortars being fired into Millstream gorge, done to reduce the risk of shrapnel flying back at the soldiers.

After an ice-cold schooner of XXXX at Ravenshoe Hotel, my intention was to go to Tully Falls but I was sidetracked. The drive along the narrow bitumen road towards Tully Falls, passing through thick lush rainforest, is a drive I shall never forget, but the falls would have to wait until tomorrow for I could not resist the walk to Charmillin Falls.

I am so glad that I was weak in the face of the sign for the walk, for it was an absolute delight. Picture thick rainforest, a good track, brush turkeys, cool air and a small waterfall of the purest quality and dimensions. It blew me away. I would dearly love to do it again, with someone, for to share the experience with another, or to spot a cassowary, would be the only possible ways to improve it. Perhaps in another life.

One can return to the car the same way, which I have a mental aversion to doing, or return via the road making a five-kilometre circuit walk. It is a little ripper of a walk.

No cassowaries yet! I had hoped to see one in the rainforest, on day one. I'm sure everyone does. I stupidly felt somewhat disappointed because I truly thought I had passed through prime cassowary real estate, but, as in most things, there is no guarantee, no entitlement, and on this day it was not to be. I hoped for a change of fortune on another day.

I camped for the night just outside of the Tully Falls National Park in a patch of semi-cleared bush away from houses. It might have been private property; it is hard to tell sometimes. There was a wire fence of sorts that had been trampled down but no signs warning that trespassers will be shot. It was getting late and I was desperate. It was already a common scenario and would continue to be for the entire trip.

Day 10

I have already touched on the road to Tully Falls and the next day, day ten, I went all the way. It is a desperately beautiful drive and I say that because, as I slowly drove along, I did not want it to end. My right foot simply refused to press any harder. Enticing signs telling of the Misty Mountains Walking Track sent my salivary glands into a frenzy of activity bordering on mania. I didn't want these moments to pass, I wanted to stop time, I wanted it to go on and on and on, perhaps forever, and I wanted to take it all in somehow. I wanted to savour every essence, cram every drop into a bottle, shove the cork in and take it with me to have for evermore.

Some of you probably remember the Claytons ads: the drink you have when you're not having a drink. Well, I'm sorry to say that the Tully Falls are like that; the falls you have when you're not having a falls. The water only plunges the 250-metre or so drop to the spectacular gorge below during the wet season; the rest of the time, the water is entirely diverted for hydroelectricity production. So there I was, at the lookout, having looked forward to seeing the falls I had often heard spoken of, staring at bare, dry rock and an annoyingly stationary pool of water immediately above where all the action should have been. The only thing falling was my excitement. Such are the disappointments of life that make one reluctant sometimes to let oneself get too carried away by anticipated excitements.

A little crestfallen, I nevertheless decided to make the best of the unforeseen situation. It is worthwhile walking to the lake above the falls from where, with a little rock-hopping, you can get to the top of the falls and look down into the spectacular gorge far below. There are no warning signs or barriers, so it is only in the alleged sense that I did the walk and I would in no way recommend it to others as it is potentially lethal. One false step and there is no hope; you will be a mangled carcass at the bottom of a very deep gorge, so please be careful and, more importantly, don't sue me if you die.

Later, I took a back road to Millaa Millaa, the scenic route as it is signposted and which entirely lived up to the description. This narrow rustic road leads you through small patches of rainforest but mostly it acquaints you with quintessential bucolic countryside, dairy country, where green hills roll on by and cows graze all day and inventive farmers turn old microwave ovens into letter boxes. It reminded me so much of South Gippsland, back home, that when I came upon a dozen or so wind turbines, I could have sworn I was approaching Toora.

The small park in Milla Milla was the perfect place to stop for lunch. There stands a statue of Palmerston, a big name in these parts, and Pompo, with the epithet of 'Explorers of the Rainforest'. The inscription, written by the Eacham Historical Society, states that 'Christie Palmerston in 1882 was the first European to find and make a feasible track through the 90 kilometres of continuous rainforest between Herberton and what is now Innisfail. The present Palmerston Highway, named in his honour, closely follows the original track.' Palmerston is also credited as the first European to climb Mt Bartle Frere (Queensland's highest mountain).

Pompo, a teenage Aboriginal, is described as his companion for over five years. I presume that Pompo's local knowledge made him an invaluable guide but what is meant by the term companion is not detailed. There is an article I read which attributes sinister activities and motives to Palmerston in general and towards Pompo in particular but I'll say no more on the matter for the facts are obscure to me and no references are listed. I'll leave the matter to historians. The inscription concludes by saying that 'Palmerston had an amazing ability not only to find his way through the rainforest but also work with the Rainforest Aboriginals. His writings on the subject have proved a valuable resource for anthropologists as his explorations were at the time.'

On to Malanda, in the heart of dairy country, where I passed a happy hour or so at Malanda Falls. This waterfall, on the North Johnstone River, is not notable, merely a short wide drop over a basalt ledge, but once more the rainforest is superb. It is possible to see Lumholtz's tree kangaroo and, in the river, platypus and snapping turtles. I saw none of those but I did see some wallabies or small kangaroos on the ground along the one-kilometre rainforest walk as well as magnificent trees towering up to the canopy above. But, yet again, no cassowaries! I was rapidly developing a no-cassowary complex.

Such an environment renders it possible for the mind to wander into the dread catacombs of life's creation, with all its extraordinary diversity and complexity. How life came about completely baffles me. I can accept neither that it is the work of a creator nor that it occurred merely by chance over billions of years. What does that leave, then, to explain life? Nothing.

If it is possible for the animate to exist merely by chance, plying its craft over a long enough period of time, then why do we not see, just as readily, the occurrence by pure chance of the inanimate. For example, being as I am in the process of building a house, why do we not see the random occurrence of concrete house stumps; surely far less complex and therefore more likely to occur if the result is only by chance? Is it simply because the inanimate cannot reproduce? I simply do not get it.

It seems to me as if atoms and molecules are somehow driven towards the creation of the animate as opposed to the inanimate but how could that be so? I understand and accept the theory of evolution as an agent for change but I do not understand what brought about that first crucial step from lifeless to life.

Perhaps the elusive answer lies somewhere in the realm of quantum biology. Perhaps the interchangeable existence of matter and energy is meaningless without life, perhaps the entire universe is meaningless without life, but is not life itself essentially meaningless? And anyway, what can possibly exist to recognise and act upon such philosophical mind-benders? Enough of this nonsense; I must put a stop to it before my head implodes.

In a deep state of confusion once more, I proceeded to Atherton, with its surrounds dominated by the sugar cane. Somewhere in its vicinity, tea is also grown but I did not see it.

Mareeba is a large town with some points of interest. It is the home of the Australian Coffee Centre, there is a mango winery nearby and it was also once the home of the now defunct North Queensland tobacco industry. The old tobacco co-op building still stands, signs and all, and it instantly reminded me of Myrtleford, where I worked for sixteen years, which was the home of the Victorian tobacco industry, located in the Ovens Valley. It too still has its large co-op shed which I believe has finally been sold to the next big industry in the region: hops.

I wish tobacco was good for you. I wish it cured cancer instead of causing it. I wish it had life-giving properties and was jam-packed with essential vitamins and minerals and all the nutrients necessary for survival and good health. I wish it was loaded with antioxidants that rejuvenated people. I wish it wasn't addictive. In essence, I wish it did the exact opposite of what it really does because I enjoy the very occasional puff of a cigar, especially with a whisky, and I would love to smoke a pipe. My fifth-grade teacher used to smoke a pipe in class and I still remember the wondrous smell of the pipe smoke. But 'tis not the case. Tobacco is a killer; there's no getting around that fact, it kills and maims and besides, if it was healthy, it would have a bad name.

Still holding to the mistaken belief that I was heading into a perilous wilderness, I filled all four of my jerrycans with precious diesel in Mareeba. As it turned out, it was a futile exercise as there were servos everywhere in the cape, but it did save me a few dollars by stocking up on cheaper fuel. Having done that, I moved on, finding a large free campground by the side of the road, chock full of nomads, just north of Mt Molloy. There was barely room to swing a cat; perhaps that is why I didn't see any and why several brush turkeys could wander about the campsite unmolested, in search of an easy feed. I threw them some sultanas, which they relished.

Day 11

I instantly fell in love with Cooktown, every piece of it: the history, art, walks, beaches, the lighthouse, the views, the pub, the plant nursery, the architecture, the Endeavour River estuary, and the superb botanic garden. What's more, I found the perfect spot to camp just out of town, in the bushland adjacent to Keating's Lagoon. What a find it was!

It was my first time in Cooktown but I had wanted to go there for years mainly because of its association with James Cook and the extraordinary voyage of the *Endeavour* but also because of its remoteness and the intriguing lure of its orchid.

The road to Cooktown is now fully sealed, which came as a pleasant surprise as the old road atlas of mine showed a long section as being dirt. Along the way to Cooktown, I stopped at a lookout, to take in the view, certainly, but mainly because nature was calling most insistently. The views were fine and the signs most revealing about some of Cape York's history including the Kennedy expedition, the Jardine expedition, and the gold rush.

The surveyor, Edmund Kennedy, was born in Guernsey and came to Australia to work and explore. He had already explored parts of inland northern NSW and southern Queensland when he set off on his ill-fated third expedition to explore Cape York. The plan was to travel up the east coast of the cape to the tip then come down its west coast to the bottom of the Gulf of Carpentaria and from there return to Sydney via an inland route. It was a sanguine undertaking that, with hindsight's benefit, seems pure folly.

On 28 April 1848, twelve men led by Kennedy left Sydney and sailed north to Rockingham Bay, near Cardwell, on the east coast of northern Queensland. There they disembarked to commence their journey by land to the tip where a waiting ship would resupply them for the next stage but, almost immediately, they got into trouble due to thick rainforest, rivers, lagoons, swamps and mountains which made progress extremely slow. Carts had to be abandoned because of the terrain and their tardiness meant that they missed the supply ship *Bramble* which awaited them at Princess Charlotte Bay.

Having seen a fair bit of rainforest by now, I can understand why the explorers had so much difficulty and the idea of trying to penetrate the rainforest with carts seems laughable.

From there, progress deteriorated further as men and horses began to weaken. Eight men were left behind at Weymouth Bay. Another three men were left in the vicinity of Shelburne Bay when one of the men accidentally shot himself, leaving only Kennedy and his Aboriginal companion Jackey Jackey to continue. The three men, Costigan, Luff and Dunn, were never seen again.

Finally, near Escape River and still about thirty kilometres from the tip, Kennedy was speared by Aborigines and died in Jackey Jackey's arms. The latter displayed incredible endurance to reach the tip and the supply ship *Ariel* alone, taking ten days to cover the distance.

Returning to Sydney, the ship stopped at Shelburne Bay but the three men were not found. Then, stopping at Weymouth Bay, only two of the eight men were found to have survived, William Carron and William Goddard. The failed expedition finally came to an end when the three survivors reached Sydney in May 1849.

The well-to-do Jardine family were living in Rockhampton when in 1864 the father, John Jardine, was appointed by the government of Queensland to establish a settlement near the tip of Cape York. This extraordinary undertaking led to the formation of the small town of Somerset, east of the tip, remnants of which can still be seen today (more on that later).

Two of John's sons, Frank and Alexander, were tasked with driving a large herd of cattle from Rockhampton to Somerset via an inland route to support the new frontier town. The expedition left Rockhampton in May 1864 and did not reach Somerset until March 1865. Ten heavily armed men, six whites and four native police, with forty-two horses, drove 250 head of cattle but, not surprisingly, their progress was slowed by the terrain and the local Indigenous peoples.

On reaching Somerset, having travelled through much country not previously explored by white man, the ten men were in poor condition. Their animals were down to twelve horses and fifty head of cattle and they had left a trail of over 200 dead Aborigines behind them! For their troubles, Frank and Alex were elected fellows of the Royal Geographical Society and received the Murchison Award in 1886.

The gold rush in Far North Queensland has its origin in the official exploration of the interior of Cape York by William Hann in 1872. He found and named the Tate, Daintree and Palmer Rivers. The Daintree was named after a pastoralist, Richard Daintree, who was running livestock in partnership with William's father, Joseph. Hann and his party found traces of gold in the Palmer and reported it to the authorities. On hearing the news, James Venture Mulligan led a party of six prospectors which set out from Georgetown in June 1872 for the Palmer. They returned three months later with 102 ounces of gold, and the rush was born.

Cooktown is not a large town. It is the perfect size for me. The first thing I did on arriving was to park at the far end of the road and walk the full length of its main drag, taking in its monuments to Cook and other things. The day was perfect for a leisurely exploration: warm, sunny, windy and beautiful.

The first monument I saw was a statue sculpted by Stanley Hammond. It shows Captain James Cook, in uniform, standing upright with legs apart as if on the quarterdeck, with a rolled-up chart in his left hand and what looks to me like a telescope in his right. His countenance is serious and determined and wholly appropriate for the scripture below which proudly proclaims that HE LEFT NOTHING UNATTEMPTED. Quite true of a European who, apart from the poles, barely left a square centimetre of the unknown world at the time for anyone else to discover.

A large monument with a tall pillar commemorates the place where Cook landed on 17 June 1770. The scripture states, *POST CINERES GLORIA VENIT*, which beautifully puts into Latin a commonplace truism of life: glory comes after one has been reduced to ashes. Cook didn't land here to see the sites, for the course into the estuary is strewn with reefs and sandbars, treacherous at any time for the unfamiliar but especially so in the age of sail. He came because he had to, to repair his ship after it struck what is now called Endeavour Reef some twenty-six nautical miles to the south-south-east. HMS *Endeavour* struck the submerged reef at around 2300, in the dead of night, on 10 June 1770 and stuck fast. It must have been terrifying, for the odds were heavily in favour of them all perishing.

As she struck near high water, the only way to free her was to jettison everything that could be spared, including rock ballast, most of the cannon and a heavy anchor. Finally, at high tide the following day and with the benefit of a calm sea, she was hauled off.

When stuck, the leakage was small and could be dealt with using a single pump but, once free, the leakage increased to such an extent that the three working pumps couldn't keep up. The water kept pouring in through the hole gouged in the timbers of the hull by the jagged coral and only muscle could pour it back out again. Everyone took turns to operate the pumps, even the aristocratic Banks.

It was a desperate situation. Barring a miracle, death surely grinned and spread its arms to welcome them to its fold in but a short while. I can imagine them working, straining, desperate, picturing loved ones, and each of them with the same unspoken thought.

She made for land, under a light breeze, but might never have reached it but for the device of fothering, suggested by midshipman Munkhouse, who had seen it done before, whereby a sail is passed under the ship and pushed into the hole by the pressure of the water, forming a seal which greatly reduced the leak to the point where it could be managed by a single pump. 'This fortunate circumstance gave new life to every one on board.' (Quote from Cook's journal.) Oakum, wool and manure had been applied to the sail to greatly increase its plugging effectiveness.

They proceeded slowly northwards, searching for a harbour into which they could stop and effect repairs. The plug continued to work effectively so that the main concern was no longer the leak but running aground or striking another reef. Boats were sent ahead to sound the depth, watch for reefs and search for a suitable place to shelter. It would seem that providence delivered the mouth of the Endeavour River, which was found on 14 June, but the winds were too strong to attempt entrance to the harbour until the 17th. As it was, she ran aground and didn't make a proper landing, at a steep beach on the southern shore, until the following day. They remained for many weeks before the ship was ready to sail again and, in that time, had mostly peaceful relations with the local inhabitants.

Later in the day, I drove up to Grassy Hill to see the lighthouse. What can I say? It looks like a lighthouse, painted in the classic colours of white with a vivid red top. It is not large; its diminutive size makes it seem more in the category of cute, I would say, rather than imposing.

While there, I read a sign labelled 'Cook's Lookout', from where, 252 years ago, Cook and Banks stood to survey the sea before them and decide on the best course to set to leave the harbour and continue their journey amidst the many reefs. It was an eerie feeling, standing where the two men had once stood, looking out at the same sea and seeing the obstacles in the form of sandbars and reefs that confronted them. It gave Cook 'no small uneasiness'. He decided that continuing north seemed to offer the clearest passage and, furthermore, was the only practicable route 'as the wind blows constantly from the south-east'. I can vouch for that. A south-easterly would be my constant companion along the coast.

In addition to aiding Cook, Grassy Hill has been a useful height over the years since. It had a wireless telegraph station which operated from 1913 to 1947 and a radar station set up during World War II

I spent the rest of the day wandering around town. I went into an art gallery on the main street but they had nothing that really appealed to me or to my budget. I was more delighted by finding a small plant nursery where, of course, I enquired about Cooktown orchids.

They had them, plenty of them, all small and rather steep at $35 each, but I had to have one as the perfect memento of my time in the place after which they are named. Preferable to teaspoons, tea towels and T-shirts, I should think. In fact, I bought two, in case one died, but I am sorry to report that they now seem to be both dead, from the cold I presume, as they looked sicker and sicker the further south I got on my return home. Such a shame. I do have a glasshouse at home but I didn't get them there soon enough. (As I write, I am pleased to report that one of them is alive and sprouting new growth and there is even a glimmer of hope for the other.)

Armed with my orchids, the next thing I came upon on my promenade was the war memorial. It featured a Leopard tank, and a toilet block painted in red poppies and with signs which read 'diggers' and 'nurses', which was a nice touch.

I set up camp for the night across the road from Keating's Lagoon, which is not far out of Cooktown, and was immediately welcomed by squadrons of mosquitoes which, logically enough, is the price one must pay for camping near a lagoon. The words of Banks, which I had read on a sign earlier in the day, immediately came to mind. I cannot possibly better his description of them.

> The Musquetos, whose peaceful dominions it seems we had invaded, spared no pains to molest as much as in their power, they followed us into the very smoke, nay almost into the fire, which as hot as the Climate was, we could better bear the heat of than their intolerable stings.

I felt for them. I guess they didn't have Rid.

The lagoon is a treasure. One of the prettiest bodies of water it is possible to imagine, being covered by water lilies in bloom and ringed by towering paperbarks and other trees. I took an evening stroll out to the bird hide and the picnic ground, about two kilometres all up, admiring the beauty and the tranquillity of the place but also on edge as there was a sign in the car park indicating recent sightings of crocodiles in the lagoon. It is extraordinary how heightened the senses are when there is even the remotest possibility of becoming prey, especially with the fading light adding to one's sense of vulnerability. I carried a big stick to wallop any croc on the head that came too close but fortunately had no cause to test its effectiveness.

I survived. I didn't see any crocs. I lived to see the fading glow of light on the water, the vivid whiteness of the water lily flowers enhanced by the twilight and the jacanas hopping from pad to pad for a late supper. It was a privilege to spend the time there.

I finally went to sleep that night but the contented smile on my face was only achieved by a concerted mosquito cull brought about by an effective search and destroy mission with a yellow plastic fly swatter.

Day 12

The next day, the twelfth, began with a visit to the botanic garden in Cooktown. For the plant lover, it is a must; for the rest of you, well, what can I say except that I hope I don't bore you too much with plant talk.

It is easily one of the best small town botanic gardens I have seen, not just for the plants but also for the information provided and the art gallery which is attached to the shop and café. Three hours of meandering and observation passed very quickly. Many of the plants I was unfamiliar with, such as the extraordinary vanilla orchid, which grows up the trunks of trees in a perfect zigzag. I had no idea that vanilla beans come from an orchid plant endemic to Mexico. I am further indebted to the land of the sombrero and taco.

The art gallery featured superb works by a local Aboriginal painter, Tulo Gordon. There were also numerous plant drawings by Parkinson, the *Endeavour*'s artist, of specimens collected by Banks and Solander, as well as plant paintings by well-known local artist Vera Scarth-Johnson.

My next destination was the Cooktown Museum, housed in the grand nineteenth-century building of the former Sisters of Mercy school and convent. There was much about Cook and the *Endeavour*, of course, but also a great deal of historical information about the town, the Indigenous people, the gold rush and the convent itself. The highlight for me, as I'm sure it is for many people, was to see one of the anchors and one of the cannons from the *Endeavour*, which had been tossed overboard during those desperate hours to save the ship, to be subsequently recovered from the sea floor and restored. History can be very moving and to see those original pieces from that famous voyage sent a shock of wonder through me.

I spent what was left of the afternoon going to Endeavour Falls which is about thirty kilometres from Cooktown. There is a roadhouse and caravan park there and the short track to the falls, no more than 300 metres, necessitates a walk through the park. It is a small park, nice and well maintained; it was quiet too, at least while I was there, and the bucket of hot chips I couldn't resist buying at the roadhouse shop, when I went in to enquire the whereabouts of the track, went down very well. It would be a good spot to spend a few nights if you want to relax somewhere out of the way.

The falls stretch across the full width of the river but the drop is only about three to four metres. I've seen better, many times; probably most times in fact. It was OK but the chips were better, just needing a little extra salt, whereas the falls needed more water and more height.

I returned to Keating's Lagoon for the night. I could think of nowhere better to stay and the mosquitoes made great company. I should add that, as a rule, I hate killing things but I am completely merciless with anything that wishes to suck my blood.

Day 13

The following morning, day thirteen, held absolutely no superstitious dread for me. What's more, I had no intention whatsoever of resisting another walk along the lagoon, crocs or no crocs, on the basis of just another integer; however, I did manage to find a sturdier stick, more of a log really, just in case there was something in it after all. This time I took photos, making good use of the inspiring early morning light. The water lilies dazzled and, once more, I watched the comb-crested jacanas hop and skip amongst the pads and flick over their edges in search of little critters to eat.

It was warm and humid and showers passed by from time to time on their way to elsewhere. It was a morning to swim and I definitely felt like one. I decided to tempt fate once more and put the theory of the thirteenth to the test to see for myself, once and for all time, if there really is anything in it after all. If it truly is a harbinger of doom, then this was to be its perfect opportunity to prove it. I drove to Quarantine Bay and walked its full length, to and fro, so that no crocodile out there could have any excuse for not seeing me except, perhaps, for cataracts, and then plunged into its cool water. It wasn't a long swim but it was refreshing and long enough, according to me at least, to disprove that thirteen is unlucky, as I confidently emerged from the water with goosebumps, certainly, but not a tooth mark to be found anywhere on my body. But I know how the minds of such believers work. They would say I was lucky because it wasn't a Friday or that it was merely a one-off and yet, if I had been eaten, they would trumpet it as clear and indisputable proof and forever tag me as a fool for ignoring the truth of what they preach as well as being thoroughly deserving of what I copped.

Having emerged from the toilet block, dried and dressed, I spied a vivid yellow flower (bear with me, plant haters!) on a nearby tree situated around the high-tide mark. The tree was of no great stature but in addition to the ostentatious flower it had a most striking reddish flaky bark. I later identified it as a red beech, *Dillenia alata*, and it, along with the previously mentioned bat's wing coral tree, became my favourite botanical discoveries of the trip.

After dicing with both fate and death and emerging victorious, I felt like another walk and Cooktown handsomely obliged with some charming tracks. After another waltz through the botanic garden, I took one that I picked up at the rear exit of the garden, and followed it to Finch Bay, with its mangrove-lined estuary, then on to Cherry Tree Bay, where I had my first encounter, on this trip, with coconut palms, before climbing Grassy Hill, seeing the views once more, then returning to the botanic garden via some of Cooktown's back streets. It was a pleasing six-kilometre walk and the numerous climbs made it a good workout to boot.

By the end of all that, it was beer o'clock. It was beer weather too, warm and humid, that makes a chilled lager go down so well. I stopped in at the Cooktown Hotel, where I had a pint of XXXX while watching the pool comp to its dramatic conclusion and chatted to a couple of the locals. They were park rangers and when asked, I made the fatal mistake of admitting that I was a retired GP. One of them, an Aboriginal man, promptly raised the subject of the trouble his haemorrhoids were giving him. He was a fair way gone by that time – referring to his degree of sobriety, not to his haemorrhoids – and he asked me what could be done about them.

Someone had earlier raised the subject of how gutless young people are these days, supposedly; you know, the old yarn about how they can't cope with anything, no resilience et cetera. I'm not sure how we'd got onto that but it is the sort of topic that is likely to crop up after a few drinks, amongst other things, often more bizarre things. Anyway, after we had all nodded our agreement about the flaws of today's youth, just as every mature generation would have done before us, this mature gent with the haemorrhoids became just as gutless as anyone else, young, middle-aged or old, when I suggested that he might need a colonoscopy. He freaked, would not have a bar of it and all I could do was laugh and point out his own hypocritical gutlessness. It was an amusing conversation at the Cooktown Hotel.

It seemed at the time like a good way to finish my time in Cooktown before word got around that I gave free consultations – leave on a high and all that. Besides, I was getting sick of the wind and the showers. So I got in the Cruiser, well under .05, I'm sure, and made my way to Lakeland, making a short detour to check out the Lion's Den pub on the way. The pub is out on its own, seemingly in the middle of nowhere; it is old, eclectic and worth a look. There is also a campground and caravan park there.

I couldn't find anywhere to camp in Lakeland, not that I had a thorough look as it was getting late, so I camped in a large clearing adjacent to the road I was travelling on, just north of town, where a side road that seemed to go nowhere took off to the left. The space was large and wide open so I got the shit blown out of me but at least it wasn't raining.

Day 14

I struck out early next morning to find a spot where I could pour my milk into my rice without the wind spraying it to Auckland. Fortune favoured me once more as I took a rough road down to the Laura River, to breakfast in the relative shelter of the valley, in riparian habitat with birds for company. I started on dinner too, cooking a stew into which I threw yesterday's leftover steak, some vegetables and a can of beans and some seasoning. It was to be a staple for the entire journey and each pot, with some bread or pasta, would do for a few dinners.

After all that, I didn't feel like stuffing around any longer. It was time to make for the heart of the cape and get on with achieving the main objective of this trip. I have to admit that by this point I was feeling the solitude and the only way to stave loneliness was to keep occupied by driving, walking, reading, writing, cooking, sleeping and by liberal dustings of social media.

The flat country became more hilly and bushy around Laura, then, just before Hahn River, the bitumen gave way to dirt, wide dirt, generally good dirt, with the dreaded corrugations not yet bad enough to be a problem; rather, they were more like ripples at that point. They got bad further north. I hate corrugations, I hate rough roads; but it is the price you pay. I feel for my old girl and I get no pleasure out of shaking around like I'm in a cocktail shaker.

I'm still not sure if it's better to drive fast or slow over corrugations – different people say different things. I tend to go slow; that was my mechanic's advice and it just seems to be my natural tendency when the going gets rough, and besides, it just feels more considerate and less injurious to the old chook, not that she's expressed any gratitude but she keeps going and that is, after all, the main thing. Besides, the partner is hard, with hard suspension, which makes for feeling every bump.

The terrain flattened out again; I think so anyway, but it was hard to see far because the scrub got thick. Farms and fences seemed to have gone. It was now unfenced grazing country where dopey-looking grey or brown cows with humps and a taste for freedom wander about unrestrained. They can wander onto the road and therein lies the problem. You keep your eyes peeled and you slow down when you come to a crest or when you see them, although, I have to say, they generally stay put by the side of the road. I guess they dislike being struck by cars every bit as much as cars and their occupants dislike striking them. Many wrecks line the road and I wonder how many are the result of bovine intervention.

I noticed a couple of things in particular as I drove up this way. One was roadkill, nothing new in that, but now it was mostly small kangaroo-like animals that I wasn't familiar with and subsequently learned are pademelons. They are very cute when alive and an all too frequent miserable sight when dead.

The other was termite mounds. They are everywhere. Forget crocodiles, buffalo, cows and even cane toads; up this way, the termite is king. Once more, the monotony of the drive made my mind wander into uncharted and somewhat bizarre thoughts. This time, the subject was termites. I was much affected by the diversity in size and shape of their real estate and, by simply extrapolating from the human state of affairs, I postulated that it must be a reflection of their various socio-economic groups. Class structure is evident everywhere you look: old wood, in the form of towering old mounds anything up to four metres high with lots of wings and chambers in which to house the best of everything; new wood, with flashy new mounds one to two metres high reflecting upward mobility, space for elegant dinner parties and a need to spell out success; the working-class or the first mound buyers seeking a foot in the door with simple, no frills mounds around the half-metre mark; and finally, and generally least of all, the battlers, the poor, the oppressed, with mounds that look something like a miserable ground-floor pile of elephant dung. Such is the way with termites: class hierarchy and the divide between the haves and have-nots is very clear.

I stopped to refuel at Coen, which is a handy little town pretty much in the middle of nowhere about halfway between Cooktown and Weipa. It has a couple of servos, a general store and a pub; everything a town and a traveller needs.

There is a free campground on the Coen River just north of the town but it was completely inundated by various shades of grey and all their paraphernalia, so I did a U-turn, drove back a few hundred metres, drove down a rough track and found a spot to myself right on the river beside a glorious waterhole. I couldn't believe my luck; it felt like a miracle had just happened.

If it was indeed a miracle, then it was of the short-lived variety and if it had been luck, then its continued presence can be interpreted either way, as a continuation of the good or as a usurpation by the bad.

No sooner had I towelled off after an invigorating swim than I found, to my immense chagrin, that my bedding was wet. I'd left my ten-litre water container in the wrong place at the wrong time with its cap unscrewed. Coming down the rough track, it had tipped over and wet the lot; pillows, doona and self-inflaters. A fire was my only hope of a reasonably dry night, so I got a good one going and arranged the wet things around it. The arrangement was rushed and somewhat precarious so you can probably predict what happened next.

Suffice to say, as I sat in my camp chair staring meditatively at the hypnotic swirls of the river, I chanced to look up and saw, where there should have been only steam curling lazily into the freshening evening air, columns of smoke reaching for the heavens with alacrity. I managed to save everything to a reasonable extent so that, by trimming away the burnt bits, I could fashion reasonably comfortable, if rustic and smelly, bedding.

The self-inflaters, however (I had taped two together for extra comfort), were now reduced to their counterparts – self-deflaters. I nevertheless slept quite well, and would do so for the remainder of the trip, on bedding trimmed of its burnt bits and of any excess luxury. The smell lessened with time and with further trimming but I had to settle for tender greater trochanters until the day of a decent mattress would finally arrive.

So, luck? You can take it either way. Bad luck in the form of spilled water and a fire, although both were more due to thoughtlessness, or good luck in the form of looking up when I did and managing to at least save most of my bedding, which was indeed nothing more than luck or intuition or mysterious intervention of some kind; call it what you will. I hate to think of what might have happened if the fire had spread to my partner, who simply sat there in silence, as always, completely unperturbed.

If I was an explorer with naming rights, I would have called the sandy point on the river where I spent the night 'Incendiary Point', but alas, it shall remain nameless, I presume, and just as well too, because later I would have had a change of mind and called it instead 'Midges that bite and annoy the crap out of you Point'.

Day 15

I had decided a while back that I would go to Weipa. It was a decision that I didn't so much regret – at least I can say I have been there and even that I touched the waters of the gulf there, for the first time, at Rocky Point – but more one that sent me on a side-trip to futility.

Weipa was a fizzer. I think I had expected a place of some beauty. I had romantic notions of a town of some splendour in the gulf tropics, something like Cooktown but to the west of the cape, with the sun setting gloriously over the waters of the gulf, plunging lush rainforest into deep darkness and awaking a vibrant nightlife. What I got instead was a pragmatic town, fully geared to the adjacent Rio Tinto bauxite mine.

There's money about, in parts. The road in is largely dirt, good dirt, nice and wide and, by and large, the corrugations are a cakewalk. There are roadworks, sections of bitumen, new bridges under construction and I expect it will be bitumen all the way to Weipa in the not too distant future.

Weipa was a flop. Boring as bat shit. Nothing much to do. I had a beer at the bowls club and the place was dead. The town lacks a soul. I couldn't find a decent pub, just bars at some of the resorts. It's dull, unless you are into watching tugboats at work and large ships at dock being loaded with bauxite, I presume. Or perhaps you're into watching large aeroplanes flying FIFOs in and out. It would be OK with a boat, to go fishing, but then, so would a million other places.

Weipa sprawls a bit. The shopping centre is a non-event and so easily missed that I drove up and down in search of it, yawning a dozen times in the process. Once located, on a side street, I bought some food. Suspicious types hung around the car park so I cleared out as fast as I could to find a place for the night.

Weipa: not for me. It feels like an empty outer suburb. The highlight was camping on the edge of the sea, just out of town, watching the sun set over the gulf and silhouetting the docks. It was a sublime sight and the only thing about Weipa I bothered to photograph.

Day 16

The following day was once again warm and humid, although it clouded over and there were even a few showers in the afternoon. Thank you, La Niña. It made driving pleasant, with the windows fully open letting in cool air and compensating for the fact that the partner doesn't have an air con.

I was getting seriously north now and the corrugations, in parts, were becoming diabolical, especially along the southern section of the Bamaga Bypass Road, an upgraded alternative to the Old Telegraph Track, the latter being, in my opinion, mostly undriveable (more on that later). There are some sections of bitumen to allow for overtaking but they seem to trigger some sort of reflex response in the pea-brains of slow drivers, causing them to speed up and not let anyone overtake them. Clearly, there is nothing that can be done for them; it is irrational and incurable. Forget fines; they should be shot on the spot, not for slow driving on rough roads, for I do that myself, but for not letting vehicles through when the opportunity arises. It makes no sense other than to reveal to all their total lack of consideration.

Having thus dispensed with another small pet hate of mine, I will now resume normal programming. I passed numerous car wrecks, as usual, and densely populated, never-ending suburbs of termite mounds, and rainforest, where it started to rain on cue, and a wondrous heathland, on a plateau, whose collection of flora must have been remarkable. But I kept going, keen to get to Fruit Bat Falls to rid myself of the dust of the road and the slime of the humidity with a most anticipated swim. I stopped at nothing to reach the cool waters.

Once there, I had to laugh. Any lingering thoughts I had that I was journeying into wilderness were whitewashed once and for all. The car park was full and I had to eke out a park by the side of the road a little way back up the road in. Kids were yelling. People were everywhere. I didn't care. All I wanted was a swim, then, in one of those sublime moments that simply seem to occur at random from time to time, I made the short walk down to the falls, the showers passed, the sun emerged and most people were going the other way, leaving the waterhole with hardly anyone in it. It could have just as easily been the opposite. It felt like a win.

I wasted no time, plunging three metres from a rock into the fully transparent water below. The sticky layer of red dust was instantly gone and I was resurrected the moment I was fully submerged; clean, refreshed, cooled and baptised back into the sensual world of nature. I showered under the falls and swam about lazily. It was marvellous.

I emerged, wrinkled and contented, after an hour or so and it was only after I'd towelled and dressed that my mind turned to the daily recurrence of the same quandary: where to stay the night. The campground at the falls was out of the question, full as a Christmas stocking. The usual permit is required and it is probably necessary to book at least three years ahead. Any cleared space anywhere in the vicinity of the falls was at a premium and taken.

I hoped to find something where you turn off the Bypass Road onto the Old Telegraph Road to get to the falls but many souls had had the same idea and everything remotely like a campsite was taken there too. There was nothing for it but to scrounge out a spot in the bush a little further on, something I was becoming quite expert at doing. It is a great advantage in these parts, especially at this time of year, not to be fussy where one plonks oneself for the night.

The plan for tomorrow, day seventeen, was to make straight for Eliot Falls and Twin Falls, a little further along the Old Telegraph Track, and then continue a bit further north to take a turn-off to the left to link back up with the Bypass Road. I was interested in exploring a bit more of the old track but not at the risk of destroying the old gal or myself, so I would play it by ear and see how it panned out and keep my options open and make use of any other cliché you care to mention that delays the final decision. I am a great believer in options and a renowned wrecker of even the best laid plans. It was a fine plan but, sadly, one that soon joined the litany of plans in my life that have become unplanned.

Day 17

The section of the Old Telegraph Track between Fruit Bat Falls and Eliot/Twin Falls is certainly rougher and a harbinger of all conceivable disasters, with deep ruts, washouts, holes and bad corrugations in some sections.

The swimming was even better at Twin Falls. The waterhole immediately below the falls is smaller than the one at Fruit Bat Falls and it was quite crowded but if you go downstream a short way, you will come to a delightful stretch of deep water, perfect for plunging into and drifting downstream, allowing the water to caress you in any direction it wishes. It is a great feeling to jump in from the rock ledges above. The water is so clear that it is impossible not to see any submerged dangers. It is also a great feeling to simply drift with one's eyes closed and just feel the cool water and the push of the current buffeting you along.

Eliot Falls are nearby and the chute at the top of them into which water is funnelled, creating a turbulent cauldron, is a sight to behold.

The invigorating swim put me in the mood for a challenge; perhaps even made me a little foolhardy if not reckless, which erased any timorous thoughts I may have harboured to go back the way I had come in. I would explore more of the Old Telegraph Track, come what may. Tally-ho! Let me tell you now, it was a bad decision, as many decisions seem to be that involve an element of bravado.

I reiterate, I have negligible experience of rough terrain four-wheel driving, I am not a petrol head and my partner lacks a snorkel, bullbar, winch and guts. It was OK at first. I remember thinking that it wasn't so bad and what was the big deal and what was all the fuss about. I was feeling good and dangerously gaining confidence. I felt like I could handle anything the road cared to throw at me.

The bravado evaporated at the first creek crossing.

I negotiated the rough narrow road down to the creek. Deep ruts threw the car from side to side. She groaned and lurched this way and that. The creek was quite deep, I'd say not far short of a metre, but the current wasn't particularly strong and it wasn't wide. The problem was that the bottom of the crossing contained large rocks that shook the car about and made progress slow. At one point, she lunged sharply and I heard and felt a sickening thud that must have done some damage, I thought, but maybe not, I hoped; she was designed for such things, I told myself, as I tried to relax my tightly wound sphincter.

I got to the other side, where some people were camping. I spoke with some of them. They all said the same thing, that the road ahead got worse and that they would turn back. Furthermore, a car had broken down a little further along and needed towing so there was a bank-up of cars with no one moving.

It was a nice spot but crowded, so I decided to turn back without further delay. However, I felt some trepidation about crossing the creek again. I'm not usually one to get very anxious but the adrenalin certainly pumped a bit when I stalled the car midstream trying to get over a boulder. The Cruiser restarted immediately and a bit more throttle saw me over the rock and onto the other side, where I felt a good measure of relief. In the midst of all this chaos, a group of buggies, it must have been at least a dozen, came through with their souped-up suspension making short work of the terrain. In fact, their suspension was so robust that the occupants seemed to float across each obstacle. Now that is the way to tackle the Old Telegraph Track if tackle it you must.

I retraced my way back to the Bamaga Road determined never to have anything more to do with the Old Telegraph Track in particular or any form of over the top four-wheel driving in general. Putting yourself and your car through all that makes no sense to me. I decided that I just don't like it.

I continued north on the Bamaga Road with the next destination being the Jardine River ferry. The old chook was running nicely, so she didn't seem to have sustained any damage. One last thing I'll say about my short stint on the Old Telegraph Track is that it made the road I was now on seem like the M1. Corrugations aside, and that's a big aside, it's a good road and often you can bypass the worst of the corrugations by slipping onto the lane that's formed by the side of the road by people with the same idea.

I reached the Jardine in good time and had lunch while waiting for the ferry to get going again, presumably once the crew had finished theirs. There is a servo, general store and camping area. You buy the ticket for the ferry at the store. Now, I am not fond of being ripped off, cash is hard to come by, and I'm sure that most of you feel the same way. But there are times in one's life when there is no way around it and this was one such time when your balls are well and truly gripped and you either grudgingly pay up or go back whence you came and they know, whoever they are, the same they who have secured a jaunty little sinecure with this ferry caper, that you haven't come all this way to see the tip only to turn back at the final hurdle because of a small-time rip-off.

The Ferry

Rotting,
Still, it charges a princely sum,
For a favour most brief
And a time in the sun.

Barely a trace of what once had been.
Did it truly sparkle?
Or merely a fancy that we see
As we would have liked it to be.

It is ascendant until its days are done,
Blessed and cursed and used.
One with the river until it is no more.
What then, when all is refused?

When old wisdom is dead
And new ideas at their zenith;
Instead of forward, do we not go back,
When we paint over the rust beneath?

So I shelled out the $110 for the return trip without a whimper. It hurt the budget but, as a tourist, you expect it. The ferry ride works out at about one dollar per metre plus GST and about one dollar per second without GST. Rather steep for a ride on a clapped-out ferry that presumably, and somewhat mysteriously, is certified riverworthy. The attendant is friendly enough. He said g'day and smiled and made mention of the fact that I was from Victoria, but that was about it as far as extras went: no tea, coffee, beer, nibbles or any other pleasantries, although, to be fair, there is scarcely time to consume anything for, in the space of a few breaths, you find yourself offloaded on the other side.

The Ferryman

The Ferryman
Is dark of skin
Which matters not,
As far as it goes.

It goes not far,
Just to the other side,
And he'll take you there
For steep talk we all know.

Between drags, he'll smile
And say g'day,
As you come to rest
On his rusted hull.

You're from Vic.
Yeah.
We get a lot. Come to get warm.
Yeah.

He tosses the butt to the Jardine
Which swirls it away,
As he too goes away.
He must work.

The ferry moves,
Rickety along its cables,
And you are there
In the time it takes to swat a fly.

In a place of two flags,
Neither your own.
A place that is unfamiliar
And white is a guest.

To a realm where its people
Are united in other ways,
That goes way back,
Instead of the cross or under the Jack.

The Ferryman is a creek,
Polluted now but still permanent,
Flowing in an eternal circle
With nowhere and no reason to go.

He dwells little on future days.
He shrugs and takes you there and back.
But he cannot take you across the great divide.
He can but toss his butt away.

The wait was about an hour before the ferry fired up again and by that time there was quite a queue. Still, I had my return ticket. I put that painful little experience behind me, and hit the road on the other side of the Jardine with enhanced enthusiasm, keen to see the very northern part of the cape.

The dirt road north of the Jardine is a lot better, perhaps thanks to ferry money, and one could easily sit on a hundred, although I prefer eighty. I had entered what is known as the Northern Peninsula Area (NPA) and in many ways it felt as if I had entered another country. It is a place that is different and a place, I suspect, with different values and priorities.

Ponies and cows wander about, seemingly to graze anywhere they have access to. Likewise, communal dogs seem to belong to no one and to everyone at the same time, and get a feed wherever they can. The cars that don't belong to tourists are mostly old and rusted and the houses are ramshackle, run-down, thrown together, with appendages made from whatever materials were available at the time. I didn't see a single dwelling that would do for a magazine cover or an episode of *Grand Designs*. I saw no evidence of people trying to keep up with the Joneses or anyone else and yet it all seemed to come together in a mysterious harmony that, to my eye at least, was not at all unpleasant.

As I am easily confused by correct etiquette and I am particularly dumbfounded by what is the current correct way to refer to Indigenous and non-indigenous peoples in this country, and given that I have a preference for straight talk that sometimes gets me into trouble, for the sake of clarity and brevity I will refer to whites and blacks. I mean no disrespect to anyone by this nomenclature; to me it is obvious and simpler. We are, white or black, all Australians, equal, or we should be, and I treat each person the same regardless of colour or ethnicity. I look at the person in front of me at the time and not at the group to which they may belong.

As I have already said, the NPA did feel to me like I had entered another country, which made it all the more exhilarating. The locals are black people, of Aboriginal or Torres Strait Islander descent, and it is they who run the place through the NPARC (Northern Peninsula Area Regional Council).

As a white person, I felt like I was a foreigner, a guest, just as you would feel when visiting any foreign country. You won't find an Australian flag there. The environment is different, the people are different, their lives are different, their language is different. They speak a form of creole or Australian Kriol, a mixture of native language and some English which, I have to admit, I couldn't understand very well at all, but the people who dealt with tourists spoke English, of course. I would recommend this marvellous region to anyone with a car that is sufficiently robust.

There are five communities, three of which (Injinoo, Umagico and New Mapoon) are Aboriginal, while the other two (Bamaga and Seisia) are Islander (source: NPA booklet). Bamaga is the main centre. You can tell because it has a large supermarket, other shops and the best-looking pub. It is also where the main NPARC office is based.

The roads between the towns are all bitumen, which made for pleasant driving and less dust. I visited Injinoo first. It is on the coast, on the gulf side. I found it very quiet, run-down and dull. There was no one about. Dogs wandered the streets. I didn't dwell. The lookout, with views across the calm waters to the Torres Strait Islands, was its best feature.

Umagico, which is also coastal and means 'black-headed python place', was next and was much like Injinoo. I briefly drove around its streets to see if there was anything of interest – there wasn't – before turning off for Alau Beach, which is just out of town.

A sign said that Alau Beach is paradise. The scepticism I have acquired through life towards any sort of claim made me have my doubts. It has a campground where I planned to spend the night. I found a spot almost on the water's edge for fourteen dollars a night. The staff were friendly. The facilities, where I had my first shower in a good while, were good. The place was packed with tourists but it wasn't rowdy. A couple of ponies and a few forlorn-looking dogs wandered about for handouts. After dinner, I took my camp chair and sat on the beach to watch the sun go down over the distant islands. Storm clouds gathered to the south and out to sea and one could see patches of showers in the distance but here it was dry and still, very still.

The leaves on the trees were motionless and the sticky humidity began to recede with the going down of the sun. The clouds messed up the sunset but it wasn't a blemish, it was simply as it was, and the sight was dramatic, almost sinister. What struck me most of all was the tranquillity of the sea.

The Arafura seemed sluggish, viscous, and stubbornly refusing to be harried by any element. There were no waves, only wavelets no more than three inches high which lapped the sand with a tinkle. I listened to the wavelets for some time, amazed that such a large sea could give rise to such small waves. As the light faded, and the sun set on another day, I sat there, mesmerised, and unable to break the spell which seemed to chain me to my chair. It was a sight and an experience I shall never forget. I found myself in total agreement with the sign I had seen. Scepticism went the way of the sun. Alau Beach is, indeed, paradise.

Before I went to bed, I decided that I would try green ants. It was the perfect opportunity as they were everywhere and seem to have a particular liking for taps and walking on hoses, using them as roads. I had heard that their abdomens contain citric acid and give the mouth a tingle when eaten so, for the record, I tried a few and can confirm that my mouth did tingle for a moment or two but this small gratification hardly justified the supreme sacrifice those small critters paid. I feel guilty now.

I slept very well that night, so the guilt cannot have been too bad. Perhaps citric acid has sedative properties. Anyway, it was the sleep of the clean and content.

The following day, the eighteenth, was to be the momentous one as well as being jam-packed with other activities as it turned out. Before leaving Alau, I returned to the beach and sat for a while, staring out once more over the calm sea, unmolested by wind or waves or living things, the latter including crocodiles. Later, however, a heron came along and I watched for a while as it stalked in the shallows amongst some nearby rocks, stealthily looking for a feed of fish. It was unsuccessful and flew off after a time in search of fishier waters but I enjoyed watching its graceful movements.

Day 18

First, I went to Seisia, not stopping at New Mapoon. Seisia, whose name rather interestingly is derived from the first letter of the names of the six brothers who founded the community of Islanders, struck me as the nicest town, right on the water, with a jetty from which tours for the islands depart and people fish. I considered doing what seems to be a bit of an iconic tour, the Three Islands Tour, but it was $275 and I didn't feel like doing it alone. It is a one-day trip by boat to Horn, Thursday and Roko Islands. It sounds amazing and I sort of regret not doing it but that bit of spilt milk is now consigned to the what-could-have-been pile and remains for evermore not to be cried over.

Seisia has a 'holiday park' but it isn't on the water. I didn't stay long because there was much I wanted to do with the day, and the tip, or Pajinka as the locals know it, was forefront in my mind. Nevertheless, I made the short detour on a dirt road to see Loyalty Beach. It too, just like Alau, has a campground on the water's edge but it is a tiny bit harder to get to. Yet again, I sat on the beach, transfixed. I watched another heron, or perhaps the same one, in the shallows, going through the same motions but also catching nothing. I watched a small black chopper land on the beach and depart fifteen minutes later and I watched the placid sea dribble in to the shore.

I went back, through Bamaga, to pick up the road to the tip. You could call Bamaga the capital city of the NPA. It has the largest commercial precinct with a sizeable supermarket and other shops including a bakery that looked pretty busy. I made note of the Bamaga Tavern, not flash but I'm not into flash, and determined to return for a drink at some point. It is also the administrative and services hub with the head office of NPARC, a hospital, health centre, pharmacy, Centrelink, police and ambulance stations and a post office. The airport is a little out of town along a sealed road.

From Bamaga, I took the road to the tip, which is dirt and takes you through sections of rainforest and eucalypt forest. I gave the Croc Tent at Lockerbie a miss but I did turn off to Punsand Bay to have a look at the resort there and check out the Corrugation Bar, 'the most northerly bar on the Australian mainland'. The resort is more upmarket than any other I had seen in the NPA and it is stunningly located. Picture rainforest only metres from the best beach I had seen so far, cool shade, comfortable outdoor facilities including a pool and an open bar, with music playing. It is definitely a step up but it was the cool shade and music that captivated me most and, had the place not been fully booked, I would have assuredly stayed the night. Hence, it was with a feeling of being hard done by that all I could do was to drown my sorrows in a chilly XXXX beer at the most northerly bar in Oz before parting ways.

The beer and the tip soothed my frustration; a new frustration added to a recurring old one. This new source of grief, which would be the only time on this trip I would experience it, was that I had not booked a night or two at Punsand; but it was an impossibility, for I knew not in advance where or when I would be at a particular time or place, as well as going against the prime ethos of the trip, which was no planning, no constraints, maximum freedom, and a search for utopia.

The recurring grief was one that I had already felt so many times, and would continue to feel many times more, brought on by seeing beautiful beaches that it was most unwise to swim in. It is more than an annoyance; it induces a pain that stings somewhere deep in the psyche, leaving you deflated. The cold beer and my brief time in these exquisite surrounds would have to suffice, that and the pinnacle moment of getting to the tip, which was now so close.

I returned to Lockerbie and once more gave the Croc Tent a miss. I let my imagination save me the cost of entry as I didn't think it would be my thing. I thought it would be a croc of…well, you know.

North of Lockerbie the road is narrow but good, apart from a single creek crossing which is a bit rough. One drives through large sections of rainforest and, at one point, on the left, I passed a turn-off to Roma Flat, which got me thinking. This is further proof that Roman legions invaded this land some two thousand years ago and struck out for the interior of what is now Queensland in search of new farming land to grow grapes and olives. They finally settled around what is now Roma but back then would have been called Nuova Roma. For some reason, this facet of our history has been covered up but it is evident in so many Italian names and people of Italian descent being in Queensland.

For those gullible enough to believe this fairy tale, it is a joke, and another example of how my deranged mind goes haywire at the slightest trigger. Then again, maybe it is true.

The road continues to a fork, the left takes you to the tip and the right to what remains of Somerset. I took the left and felt a thrill and a growing sense of achievement as I drew closer and closer to the main object of my travels. The red dirt road became a red carpet and the thick rainforest on either side became a green, visual fanfare as I slowly made my way along to the imaginary cheer of an imaginary crowd.

There was not a trace of ostentation at the end of the road from which it is necessary and also fitting to get off one's arse and walk the kilometre or so to the tip. There were a few shacks, a few portable loos, a sloppy car park and a few campers. I loved the simplicity and understatement of the place, a far cry from some of the catastrophes, created in the name of tourist development, I would have the displeasure to encounter along the east coast. The beach is wide and flat, at least at low tide, and from its expanse one has a clear view to the west towards Punsand and east to the tip. It was warm and humid and the urge to immediately plunge into the sea had to be fought off.

I walked over the rocky hill that leads from the car park to the tip. It felt auspicious as each step brought me closer to the landmark and my goal. There was a bit of scrambling down amongst some rocks near the end of the track and then I was there, at the very tip, where the sign proclaims, YOU ARE STANDING AT THE NORTHERNMOST POINT OF THE AUSTRALIAN CONTINENT.

The Call

The call goes out,
Without device
Save receptive souls.
Insistent, persistent.

No wave or beam
Disturbed of its slumber
Nor suffered to sweat
For a transmission from within.

Resist the extremes, ignore the unknown?
Impossible,
For they are as the peals of church
Or the strains of minaret.

The call
Infiltrates every fibre
And intensifies
With each unheeded day.

It whispers at night
Or comes
Like a train from a tunnel.
Ravaging all sense.

Cook, Hilary, Amundsen, and Polo
Were all devoured until deed was done,
Then a respite
Until the next call will come.

I felt great. I felt like I had done something worthwhile and seen much of this great land in the process. For some time, I simply sat and watched the sea of Torres Strait swirl past the tip in the narrow strait between it and the small island immediately to the north. There were many other people and one of them kindly took the photo that everyone has to get, of themselves standing at the sign. As he took the photo of me, his son, I assume, suggested that it would be a great place to build a hotel. Now there's a kid to keep an eye on; hopefully he will channel his precocious entrepreneurial talents into more appropriate enterprises.

It was very hard to leave. I thought, this is it, I will never see this again. I looked at the rocks, I took a photo of the northernmost rock with the sea swirling around it, I looked at the islands and I kept looking at the sea and was fortunate enough to see a large turtle swim past only a few metres from me. It was a final reward before I turned to go.

I collected a few stones as mementos, the northernmost stones I could get my hands on, and headed back to the car, this time scrambling along the lower rocks to pick up the beach rather than going back over the hill.

I felt a sense of anticlimax as I made my way on the road to Somerset. It was to be expected, as the prime object of the trip was now behind me and from now on I would be making my way home, but there was still much to see and do along the way.

Somerset comes as a surprise in more ways than one. By its few remains, it is incredible to believe, almost impossible to believe, not only that a settlement existed here but also the height of hubris or the grandest of delusions that not only conceived the idea but that led to its creation.

According to information from the Royal Historical Society of Queensland, the governments of Britain and Queensland decided to establish the settlement, named after Lord Somerset, the First Lord of the Admiralty, to provide a refuge and supply depot for passing ships, to act as a base for the link between Australia and Great Britain via the Torres Strait and as a counter to the French naval base in New Caledonia.

Somerset was built in 1864 and John Jardine, from Rockhampton, was appointed as its first police magistrate and commissioner. He had grand plans to develop Somerset into a major port and centre of commerce, something to rival Singapore perhaps, but that wasn't to be. It seems to me, albeit with the benefit of hindsight, that the place was too remote and lacked the population base and infrastructure for such a grand vision to succeed.

I have already mentioned the now infamous inland expedition led by Jardine's sons, Frank and Alex, to bring cattle and horses to the settlement, which resulted in the deaths of many Aborigines. Over the next thirty years, Cape York's indigenous population was estimated to have fallen from 3,000 to 300 because of violence, disease and hunger.

Somerset never flourished. It rapidly went into decline in the 1870s once government institutions were transferred to Thursday Island. John Jardine returned to Rockhampton but Frank stayed on, relying on cattle, a coconut plantation and pearls for his income. He married a Samoan woman, had four children, died of leprosy in 1919 and is buried at the small cemetery in Somerset. His wife, Sana Solia, was buried at Somerset Beach where a headstone remains.

Not much remains of Somerset now. There is a small cemetery containing eight graves, three small cannons around a flagpole and a memorial cross, built in 1971, to commemorate the centenary of the coming of evangelical Christianity to the Torres Strait, and later to Papua New Guinea, by Polynesian missionaries and the Reverends Samuel McFarlane and A. Murray. In a touching statement, it marks this 'Coming of the Light' as an important occasion in the Torres Strait Islander history. I hope the changes that came with this new light, unlike the dark that was most prevalent with the coming of the Jardines, were for the good of the local people's lives.

So, with the glory of the tip and the disintegrated dreams of Somerset behind me, and following some robust internal debate, I decided to do the Five Beaches four-wheel drive track which is close by. I love beaches, as I'm sure most of you do, so, much as I was getting sick of driving, especially on rough roads, the lure was too much. I am happy to say that it was the correct decision.

It isn't a long drive, perhaps thirty kilometres, I'm not sure, but it is rough in parts and very sandy in others. In fact, late in the day, I pulled a car out of soft sand; a good deed which inflated my ego and went some way towards making me feel like a bona fide four-wheel driver.

I thoroughly enjoyed the drive. The scenery, the views, the beaches, the dunes and, yes, the challenge, which could be rated as fun, with the right vehicle, rather than over-the-top risky to car or person that the OTT was.

To cap a momentous day with the best possible finale, I found the perfect place to camp, backing my car under some trees at the very southern end of the third beach. There, I had shade to deliver me from the heat and humidity and a tiny stream for companionship as its water trickled past me on its meandering course to join its salty kin. I could not have asked for a better place nor for a better beach on which to take an evening stroll, amongst battalions of soldier crabs strewn on its wide expanse.

The Coral Sea, battered by the incessant south-easterlies, was a lot rougher than the gulf waters and the Arafura on the other side but it was very pleasant to fall asleep to the sound of breaking waves after absorbing the colours and light of the sunset and reminiscing over the events of the day.

> Bitumen, my love,
> You are a reminder yet,
> Of all things wanted
> That one cannot get.

Day 19

I woke to day nineteen after a dreadful sleep. It was warm, sticky, humid and I had accumulated a torment of mosquito bites. Adding to this misery was a layer of red dust which was all-pervasive and non-discriminatory about its preference on where to settle. Once more, I cursed the dusty roads, the corrugations and the humidity; I am a fan of none of those things and with each day my love of bitumen and cool climes reached new heights.

Nevertheless, my muttering, complaining soliloquy was tempered by the reiteration that there is always a price to be paid in achievement and my paltry discomforts were as nothing compared to those of Cook, Kennedy, the Jardines and the Indigenous peoples.

The sunrise woke me and I got up to watch its glorious rise over the sea. The morning sea was calm but not as calm as that of the gulf, on the other side, for it cannot be possible for another sea to better its tranquillity. One-foot waves rolled in and broke on the sand with a relaxing thump. They came in undisturbed, with perfect form and with metronome regularity, governed by immutable and universal mathematical laws which I cannot fathom but others can.

Before leaving, I strolled along the beach once more. The tide was up but the water was nowhere near my campsite. I was reacquainted with the red beech, for there was one not far from my camp and immediately adjacent to the trickling freshwater stream. It had found for itself a perfect location. This one was not in flower but, rather, one of its fruits had opened right up, like those of pittosporum, to reveal its intensely red interior. It was strikingly beautiful. I took a photo.

I collected some rubbish that was accumulated around my campsite but it was merely a token gesture as I quickly realised the futility of my efforts. It is most distressing to see so much rubbish on these otherwise pristine beaches, washed up to the high-tide mark, where they will stay for a very long time. It most probably originates in Asia, where I have holidayed a few times, enjoying it immensely while being simultaneously appalled by the amount of rubbish dumped anywhere and everywhere – streets, gutters, gullies and rivers – most to inevitably end up in the sea. It is a never-ending tragedy the way most humans thoughtlessly treat the natural world.

I completed the loop, driving along two more beaches, through some sections of rainforest and sand dunes, and some sections where the track is composed largely of jagged scoria protruding from the soil and itching to get at rubber. I made my way very slowly over the nasty buggers, picking the best path as well as I could to avoid a puncture as I had already seen a car with a puncture near where I had camped and changing a wheel would be a real pain in the arse for me because I didn't have the right type of jack to use on sand.

I made a quick trip to Somerset Beach just to have a look. There is a campground with basic facilities and there were quite a few people there.

I returned to Bamaga, once more avoiding the Croc Tent. I wandered around the shops and checked out the supermarket and cashed up at the ATM there. Then, bored with the same food all the time and feeling like I deserved a treat, I went to the bakery on the main street and bought a couple of danishes, which I devoured in no time at all.

The Bamaga Tavern doesn't look like much from the outside but it seems to be the go-to place in town and, being a Friday, I thought I'd go back in the evening to mingle with some of the locals over a beer or two. In the meantime, I decided to spend another night at Alau Beach as I liked it there very much, the people were friendly and you couldn't argue about the price.

I am a creature of habit over some things so, finding my previous campsite unoccupied, I staked my claim there once more. The pull of habit is not so strong, however, as to stop me from claiming a better spot if it was available, but here there was shade and it was a matter of a couple of dozen steps to the beach so there was little chance that it could be bettered.

After a much-needed shower, I sat on the beach in the small yellow beach chair I had nicked from my sister. Then I went for a long walk, south along the beach, past a couple of small rocky headlands to the wreck of a small aluminium dinghy before turning back. It was very warm, around thirty, and very humid and the usual storm clouds were brewing out to sea and dumping their showers here and there in the distance. A few heavy drops of rain fell as I had dinner, then, just on dark, I made my way to Bamaga to join some folks at the tavern.

AFL is in my blood, which flows the blue and white of the mighty Cats. I'm not a fan of rugby, although I watch the origin games when I can. But up here, in the Bamaga Tavern, it was NRL or Keno and of the two I definitely prefer NRL. I found the tavern surprisingly quiet; somewhere less than twenty people, mostly black people but a few whites, and a couple of families of obvious tourists having dinner.

I sat in a couch that I had to myself, just back from the bar, with a clear view of the TV. In a high-scoring game, the Roosters gave the Raiders a shellacking, seeming to be able to score tries at will. I watched the whole game, had a couple of pints and spoke only to the bartenders. The locals were enjoying themselves, watching the game and getting increasingly rowdy. Most of the time I couldn't understand what they were saying as they were speaking their own language, laughing loudly, and the place was noisy. After the game, as I left, one of the locals nodded to me and that small gesture made me feel really good; better than words could ever do. I felt like I had been accepted. It broke down a barrier. I nodded back.

> From wherever you're comin'
> To wherever you're goin',
> You'll find refreshment
> On the Coen.

Day 20

The weather continued to be clement. The heat and humidity, made worse by being unable to swim in the sea, distressed me. It reduced me to a state of mental and physical torpor. I could not get Twin Falls, Eliot Falls, Fruit Bat Falls and the Coen River off my mind. This mitigated the sadness I felt on leaving the NPA.

You see, there was so much about the place that I liked, climate aside, and a person with simple and inexpensive tastes could happily live there. It has the appearance at least of only one class. The towns and the facilities are simple if not ramshackle. You won't find finery or luxury there, not that I saw anyway. The houses are mostly run-down, there is not a flash car to be seen except those of the tourists, and there is neither *haute couture* nor *haute cuisine*. I don't know if the local people are fundamentally happy but my gut feeling is that they are and that they consider the place their paradise. I'm glad I came to share it for a few days.

It was a day of heat, a day of dust and a day of corrugations, 458 kilometres of them, and trying to avoid them as much as possible. I was, for the last time, reincarnated into a cooler and cleaner being at Fruit Bat Falls before pushing on to camp again on the Coen River, where I immediately had another swim. Incendiary Point was unfortunately taken so I had to settle for a lesser spot a way back from the river.

More and more, I longed for bitumen. One more day of dirt, through Lakefield National Park, then blessed bitumen for the rest of the trip.

My love for you grows, I say,
Whenever tumbles of dust come my way.
My leaves are shot,
My shockers are shocked
And my steering has rheumatics every day.

Day 21

I spent day twenty-one exploring Lakefield National Park. It was a big day as there was much to see, but before getting onto that I will try one final time to convince those who still harbour fanciful delusions of taking on the Old Telegraph Track: don't do it! If you value your car, your passengers or yourself, don't do it! It is an evil menace of the highest order and if you still must be persuaded, then perhaps you will consider these humble lines of poetry entitled

> Give it a miss.
>
> If your dear sweet darlin'
> Dislikes hearing you cussin',
> Give it a miss.
>
> If you place value
> On each and every sinew,
> Give it a miss.
>
> If your back is corroded
> And your neck is decrepit,
> Give it a miss.
>
> If each corrugation
> Makes you scream fornication,
> Give it a miss.

If crossing a creek
Makes you quake, freak and shriek,
Give it a miss.

If the state of your account
Won't mend your mount,
Give it a miss.

If each hole, gouge, or rut
Gives you a twist in the gut,
Give it a miss.

If you don't fancy your mind
Ending up in your hind,
Give it a miss.

If you don't have the cojones
To take on such hombres,
Give it a miss,

For it is no piece of piss
To fool with the devil's kiss.
Be damned, the Old Telegraph Track.

    The first stop in Lakefield National Park was at the majestic Sweetwater Lake, where I sat in the shade of a tree and with one eye looked out over the water, at the water lilies and the bird life, while the other was on sentry duty, watching for reptiles with large snouts and teeth. I didn't see any crocs, but some campers nearby, in a campground that would fit only a few tents, told me they had seen one at the lake's edge, at the very spot where I'd been sitting earlier that morning.
    The variety of birds here was extraordinary, including a pair of sarus cranes wading in the shallows. I was very excited to see them. They are

a very elegant bird and graceful in their movements. Their plumage is mostly grey but they have an outstanding red neck and head. I cursed not bringing my bird books and binoculars.

The flies were bad and the mosquitoes tormented me if I stayed too long in the shade, so I moved on, driving across Nifold Plain, a large area of open country largely devoid of trees, where you are once again reminded that in these parts, *rex termitus* is sovereign lord. Their huge mounds, disappearing into the distance and having the effect of resembling a massive cemetery full of headstones, demand to be photographed. I was stumped by what so many termites could possibly eat because I saw scarcely any wood and deduced that they must feed on grasses, sedges and shrubs; anything with cellulose will do, I suppose.

Lakefield National Park is full of swamps, bodies of water, creeks, and rivers. It must be quite a sight in the wet if it's even possible to get in there during that time. I expect that it lives up to its name then, becoming a giant lake.

I'm sure that it, like every other part of this country, it seems, has its fair share of weeds but, coming from Victoria where so many rivers and creeks are choked by blackberries, it is great to see rivers in what appears to be an essentially natural state, untarnished by this incredibly invasive and diabolical weed. So much riparian habitat in Victoria has been destroyed and made virtually impenetrable by the aggressively competitive blackberry, which manages to choke out every other plant. It smothers entire valleys and no other plant can stand up to it. Good as the berries are to eat, its introduction to this land, like so many other things, has been a disaster.

My next stop was the Red Lagoon and its magnificent lotus. The lagoon is full of pink-flowering lotus that were just beginning to flower, as well as water lilies and sedges. The tubers of bulkuru sedge are a favourite food of magpie geese, while the seeds of umbrella sedge are eaten by seed-eating birds such as finches. The breeze rustling the large lotus leaves, which can reach one metre in diameter, created a soothing, almost musical, sound which readily induces in one a meditative state but there was nothing soothing nor meditative about the squadrons of mosquitoes that descended on me moments after my arrival, aborting my visit and forcing a hasty retreat, but not before I had the joy of seeing another pair of sarus cranes creeping about in the lagoon some fifty metres away.

On to White Lagoon and its white-flowering water lilies, the experience adorned by the raucous carryings-on of the white cockatoos nearby.

Next stop was Kalpowar Crossing on the Normanby River. The crossing is a concrete roadway over which the river flows and it acts as a low dam, creating a beautiful stretch of broad river upstream. There is a large campground with good facilities, including showers, but there were very few people.

I felt like a good walk and exploring some of the country but I had trouble locating the nature trail, which is meant to follow the river. Perhaps it has been washed away or perhaps you simply make your own way along the rocks and sand and shrubs of the riverbank, or maybe I'm going blind. Whichever the case may be, I gave up after a while and returned to the campground only to find my own natural spectacular, near the river crossing, in the form of a sand monitor (goanna) swallowing a snake.

I would guess that about half the snake was already down the goanna's gullet by the time I tuned in to watch and I was immediately captivated. As the other half gradually vanished in a few minutes, I realised that I was witnessing something special and very rare and the likes of which I had never seen before. It can best be described as a spectacle of engorged gluttony as the lizard took powerful neck thrusting swallows to get his catch down. Finally, the tip of the tail vanished and I could picture the serpent doing a few final corkscrews in the goanna's stomach. I imagined that the lizard then wished to rid himself of his audience and simply bask in the sun to digest its meal in peace: relaxed, contented, satiated; immersed in a post-prandial siesta.

He turned his head to look at me and I'd swear on my mother's eyes that the expression on his face was a questioning one, as if to ask, what the hell are you staring at? Don't you have to eat too? Fuck off, will ya? I left him in peace and I assume he wouldn't need another feed for a long time. I would have given my testicles for a decent camera and a telephoto lens but, alas, I possess neither.

The last stop for the day was Laura Homestead or, to be more precise, the ruins of Laura Homestead. It was the usual thing: clapped-out sheds, rusted-out vehicles, decaying fences and a homestead of hardwood and corrugated iron slowly dissolving back into its constituent atoms. The highlights were probably a couple of huge frangipanis and a bird with a call that sounds like a sneeze. I've heard its call several times in my travels but it is a shy critter so I have yet to get a proper look at it and I have been unable to identify it. On this occasion, I did see the bird fly away but I couldn't make out any distinguishing features, merely one more small to medium-sized bird making its hasty escape, silhouetted against the sky so that it looked a nondescript grey or brown colour.

The ruins aren't much to look at now but the history is interesting. It was established as a cattle station in 1879 by an Irish immigrant, Fergus O'Beirne, to supply meat for the gold miners around Palmer River and elsewhere. The original homestead was built in 1892, subsequently improved, and was occupied until 1966.

It had been a great day. I had seen so much and I was content and my hunger for activity had been satisfied. I was tired and it was getting late and the same old problem presented itself but I managed to find a decent campsite just up from a creek crossing about ten kilometres from the national park towards Laura. I spent what remained of daylight sitting by the creek with my dinner, watching the water wander past me and small birds flitting amongst the trees and bushes.

Day 22

Today, day twenty-two, it was with a sense of great relief that I said goodbye to dirt roads.

> 'Tis a feather bed I want
> And the plushest pile I need.
> Only tar
> For me and my car
> And if the road to heaven is bitumen, that is where I'll be.

I saw the usual car wrecks by the side of the road today but also a lot of those little crosses, flowers, and other ornaments that people place at the site where a loved one has died as a result of a motor vehicle accident. It was a reminder that on the road we are only one mistake from death; and we make mistakes.

> Nowhere better
> To boast, host, and toast,
> Than the glittering east coast.

I reached Mossman in good time, without stopping. There, I did what I had to do, refuel and food shop, then I decided to go to the must-see place, Mossman Gorge. I had been there before, about twenty-three years ago, when the kids were little and we were holidaying at Port Douglas and Daintree. That was a different sort of holiday entirely: resorts, cabins, pools, sailing, scuba diving, seeing crocs and cane toads et cetera. I had good memories of Mossman Gorge, walking through rainforest on dirt tracks to get to the deep waterholes that were refreshing to swim in. I remember people, back then, but not too many. There was room to move and swim and at least in part to have a sense of being one with nature.

This time however, going to Mossman Gorge was a big mistake. It is nothing like it once was and all it took was a few moments to destroy the good memories I had of the place. It has, I'm afraid to say, become completely dandified.

The massive car park, almost full, was a bad omen. Lots of flash spotless cars was another bad omen. Things rapidly deteriorated from there; indeed, for me, spiralled downwards and completely out of control. In my sweetly innocent naivety, I got out of the dirty Cruiser, which was covered in red dust, and sauntered towards where I guessed the start of the walking track to the gorge would be. I wore an old straw hat, a moth-eaten old T-shirt with a gecko print on the front that I picked up cheap in Vietnam, an old pair of pale green shorts with tears in them (at least they were Country Road) and a pair of thongs. I enthusiastically had a towel draped across my shoulders and I'd slathered on the sunblock. All I wanted was a nice shady walk, a deep waterhole, a swim and getting the dust off me; what I got was entirely different.

As I approached, I soon gleaned that the place wasn't like it used to be and my heart began to sink. I had a bad feeling and it was getting worse with every step I got closer to the entrance. I'd seen this sort of thing before and I didn't like it. It was the dreaded tourist complex for cashed-up people who like style and comfort first and the natural world somewhere down the order of things. As soon as I entered the place, I think it was through automatic doors, I knew that I was in trouble and that the place was exclusively designed to sting the bank balance.

I walked through, stunned, in a daze and a world of disappointment. This wasn't what I'd expected. It wasn't me. Everyone looked immaculate in their best clothes. Where I'd expected the smell of trees and earth, I got perfume and aftershave. Where I'd expected birdsong and happy children squealing, I got funky music and kids on their best behaviour. Where I'd expected to see a bushwalking track, rainforest and a river, I got a café/bistro/restaurant, whatever it was, a souvenir shop/gallery and swarms of people sitting around eating and drinking. I was the only one carrying a towel!

I hate this sort of shit. People watched me with distaste and perhaps even pity. Maybe they thought I was homeless or a dero needing a wash. Maybe they thought I was a druggie as I continued my dazed progress through the complex and out of the rear exit to regain my senses only once I was outside again. I looked about for signs of a walking track to the gorge. Eureka, I found one proceeding to the left but found to my immense dismay, after following it for a very short way, that it came to an end with the all too familiar, bright red, do not enter sign. I turned back. I was at a loss. I couldn't see any other tracks, so in desperation I asked a gentleman who was seated nearby, tucking into his sloppy lunch, if he knew where the track to the gorge was. He answered with a sour look on his face, clearly not taking kindly to having his feed disturbed by a random dero. He told me that I had to go back inside, to reception, where the gift shop was.

I immediately panicked. I knew exactly what was coming. It is a sad state of affairs, at least to my way of thinking, when one has to go to reception in a plush complex to pick up a walking track to go and see some bush and a river. Fair enough if you want a room in a fancy hotel but not for a fucking walking track! I wondered what the old-timers would have made of it all, you know, all those pioneers, the drovers, the gold miners, and the Aborigines, if they saw all this shit. That we had lost the plot, I imagine, and become no better than soft-boiled eggs.

My panic got worse. I didn't want to go back inside. I had that very bad feeling in my gut again but I overcame my terror and recklessly plunged headlong for the reception counter, surrounded in all directions by merchandise, and sure enough, once there, there it was, the dreaded eftpos machine. I knew it. I knew it would cost. I knew I'd get slugged. All this fancy stuff doesn't come for free. Someone thought of turning a natural wonderland into a cash cow. Sadly, there is nothing new in that and the terrifying thought of a hotel at the tip, the brainchild of an entrepreneurial kid becoming a reality, flashed through my damaged mind.

I joined the queue, feeling like a lamb at an abattoir. I heard everything that I needed to hear when the man in front of me was served. Thirteen dollars per adult, some sort of shuttle bus and you are time-limited; you get an hour and twenty minutes up there to do whatever you want before being bussed back, I suppose. That was it, I'd heard enough. What I wanted was to get out of this place and never return. I did not stop, I did not pass go and I did not buy a single item of merchandise. I cleared out as quickly as I could and did not feel myself again until I was well clear of that cesspool.

Wandering around Mossman CBD wasn't much chop either but I found a pretty good spot to camp, next to a sugar cane plantation, screened from the road by trees, just out of Mossman on the road to the cursed gorge.

Day 23

Day twenty-three was good. First stop was Port Douglas, where I wanted to reacquaint myself with the place, reminisce a little and walk along the beach. What struck me most of all was the stark contrast with where I had come from just days before, the NPA. Port Douglas is money, elegance, resorts, golf, mansions, fine dining, fine wine and champagne, fine shopping, Mercs and Beamers. You get a sense of sparkling cutlery waltzing across fine bone china. Grand houses overlooking the water grabbed at the morning sun. There were pleasant smells, sunglasses everywhere and no roaming, hungry quadrupeds.

Walking along the beach was like driving on the Monash Freeway, only faster and more refined. The people are well-clad and image-conscious. Some are delicate; I saw a woman indecisively pussy-foot around through a trickle of water perhaps two centimetres deep, at the most, so as not to get her pristine white runners damp or marked. The in-tune reader may have gleaned that this type of place is not my cup of tea and if so then give yourself a pat on the back, for you have just gleaned correctly.

Everything, and I mean everything, was different to the NPA. The people of Port Douglas are beautiful. They walk with their poodles and labradoodles. They have two arms, two legs, one head but only one skin colour – white. You don't see black people here; at least, I didn't.

After a long walk up and down the beach, I had a brief swim in the sea to get rid of the sweat, at a place where a few other people were swimming and it was patrolled. I took care to leave a couple of other people between me and the horizon at all times, as croc or shark bait, then I left.

Next stop was Palm Cove; more of the same but not quite as flash as Port Douglas. I had planned to meet friends there but it didn't work out. I walked up and down the main street for a while hoping to bump into them, yawned a dozen times in the process and became semi-zombified before taking my leave.

I had a pleasant afternoon consisting of water and rainforest. I stopped at a small, pretty town called Babinda, walked around the town, and then met the woman at the information centre to get some, you guessed it, information. She was a talker, evidently proud of her locale, sang its praises, spruiked its assets and she was very hard to detach oneself from. She was good at her job; too good. Very enthusiastic. Many times I waited for her to pause for breath but it never came. Many times I took a step towards the exit to no avail. Many times I said, 'Well…' without effect. But she did do the good deed of convincing me to visit the Babinda Boulders, which I did straight away or, more accurately, as soon as I could extricate myself from this Medusa with a formidable tongue.

At the Boulders I saw, for the first time, a Ulysses butterfly. Its dazzling blue colour, as it fluttered its way through the valley, contrasting superbly with the lively green of the rainforest, is a sight I shall never forget and if I saw nothing else, that of itself would have made the trip to Babinda Boulders worthwhile.

But I did see other things. I saw the cool water of Babinda Creek, originating from the slopes of Mt Bartle Frere, plunge amongst a series of massive granite boulders, creating deep, perfectly clear waterholes into which some souls were jumping. I saw Golden Hole, a large majestic waterhole. I saw Josephine Falls, a sublime series of cascades, four in all if my count is accurate, the final one consisting of a six-metre rock slide into a deep pool that would shame any man-made pool I have ever seen. What I did not see was a shuttle bus, reception area and eftpos machine; I guess they will come in time.

From Josephine Falls there is a track which climbs Mt Bartle Frere, Queensland's highest mountain. Of course I was tempted, but I didn't think I would be fit enough for such a climb at the moment after several weeks of mostly sitting in the car. I'd seen the mountain as I made my way south. For such a colossus, it seemed to be very bashful, with its summit perpetually covered by cloud, unlike its namesake, Sir Henry Bartle Frere, about whom, if one were to choose a word to describe his personality, bashful would surely be last on the list.

Bartle Frere is an interesting historical figure. In the mid to latter nineteenth century, he was an administrator for the British empire. Of Welsh extraction, he had a successful career in India, becoming governor of Bombay, but it was his controversial and disastrous time as high commissioner for Southern Africa for which he is most remembered. It was his vigorous pursuit of implementing the wish of the Secretary for the Colonies, Lord Carnarvon, to confederate all southern African states under British rule which led to inevitable conflict.

He perfectly displayed the typical arrogance of British colonial officials as well as the almost universal capacity of these same officials, and the British army leadership, to consistently underestimate their foes and to exhibit extreme tardiness in recognising and implementing the necessary changes to successfully adapt to different types of warfare. Arrogance, tradition and an inability to adapt would lead to military reversals and be paid for in British blood.

Unsurprisingly, the Boers and some native African states, most notably the Zulus, were suspicious of the idea of a confederation, concerned that it was merely a way for Britain to increase its power in Southern Africa. A precursor of what was to come was Bartle Frere's opportunistic declaration of war on the black tribes, the Xhosa people, of Gcalekaland. The defeat of the Xhosa led to the annexation of their land into the proposed confederation.

As a firm believer of British colonialism and superiority, Bartle Frere saw the existence of independent African states as an ongoing threat of Kaffirdom against white civilisation. This was, in Victorian England, the accepted wisdom of the majority, at least of those in power, and the jargon of the times. Clearly, a situation where black people, or Boers for that matter, retained their independence and power was not to be tolerated, so he turned his attention next onto the Zulus. He schemed to provoke a war with the Zulus with the aim of deposing King Cetshwayo, defeating the Zulu army and annexing Zululand into the confederation.

The British army, under Lord Chelmsford, invaded Zululand in January 1879, in accordance with Bartle Frere's policy and without official British government approval! I expect that both men would have considered the war to be a mere formality and, harbouring a hefty dose of overconfidence, likely to be over in a very short time. Surely, once the Zulus had tasted British military might, they would submit and return to their farms and herds. But that is not what happened.

Once more, the British underestimated the enemy, the fierceness of the Zulu warrior in defending their own land as well as the power of overwhelming numerical superiority coupled with knowledge of the terrain. They also overestimated the capacity of the British army, even when equipped with modern weapons, to resist a force outnumbering them by twenty-to-one on open ground.

That is what happened at the first major battle of the Zulu war, Isandlwana, where, only eleven days after the invasion, a British force was wiped out. It was a military disaster of the highest order for the British, only partly made up for by the heroics at Rorke's Drift later that day, and it was a stern lesson that the Zulu were not to be taken lightly. The successful defence of Rorke's Drift was pumped up in the papers and Victoria Crosses were handed out like lollipops in order to cover up the disaster at Isandlwana.

In the aftermath of Isandlwana, Bartle Frere was censured but not recalled. The Anglo-Zulu war ended with the defeat of the Zulus, after significant British reinforcements arrived, later in the year. It came after a second invasion by a much larger British force. The British victory ensured their control of Zululand as part of the confederation of nations.

The British annexation of the Transvaal in 1877 led to growing disaffection by the Boer population towards British rule and Bartle Frere's leadership in particular. Eventually, tensions spilled over into the First Boer War of 1880–1881. It was a short-lived affair, only three months, with relatively few casualties, but the result was a decisive Boer victory which led to the British recognition of the South African Republic and the death knell of the confederation.

Bartle Frere was recalled to London in 1880, with his reputation tarnished, and died four years later. Perhaps he had ruled with his head in the clouds just as the mountain that bears his name does to this day.

I have digressed from the mountain to the man, for I am fascinated by history. I hope that the reader is not offended. At the risk of trying the reader's patience further, I have one more piece of history to tell, which I learned of at Babinda Boulders. It is of the tragic crash of a USAAF B25C Mitchell Bomber into Mt Bartle Frere on 21 April 1942.

I was much affected by this tragedy, especially on seeing the photo of the young pilot, Captain Glenwood Stephenson, next to a photo of his young and very pretty wife Anne. They had married just two weeks before Glenwood left the USA. Below the photos is a letter Glenwood wrote to Anne, the last letter he would write, eleven days before his death.

Dear Anne

I haven't much left of what I started from home with just your pictures, a raincoat and a pair of wings. And believe me sweetheart; I really treasure these pictures of you. They have been out in the jungles, through plenty of bombings raids, but I get them out the first time that I stop. Haven't been in one place over a couple of weeks since the war began. Expect to move on again tomorrow. Hope I won't be long before we're together again.

Glenwood's gold graduation ring from West Point was removed from his body and returned to Anne, who was buried with the ring when she died. It is only one of millions of such tales, from all wars, but it felt very personal to me and I was very moved. Glenwood and his six crew died on the side of a mountain a long way from home, helping to defend our country against the Japanese. I am grateful for their sacrifice and it is fitting that they are remembered in this way.

Following Japan's invasion of New Guinea, the United States decided to build an air base at Charters Towers from which to attack Japanese forces in New Guinea. It was built in March 1942. Glenwood's plane was returning from a mission in support of Australian ground forces when it encountered a severe storm as it approached Mt Bartle Frere. It crashed into the mountain and the entire crew perished.

The sign went on to say that there are 116 United States airmen known to have lost their lives in air crashes in 1942 within a radius of 250 kilometres of Babinda. Those who died on Mt Bartle Frere were Glenwood Stephenson, John Jefferson Keeter Jnr, Eugene Thomas Tisonyai, Wm H. Lancaster, Jimmie D. Morris, George C. DeArmond and James P. English. I mention their names to acknowledge their service and to respect their memory and all those who sacrificed themselves to defend this land against the threat of Japanese invasion.

Because of bad weather and thick forest, it took one week to discover the crash site. First on the scene were Lido Poppi, Iva Vicaroli and Jimmy Safioti, all local residents.

I decided to spend the night at nearby Bramston Beach. On the way there, passing through the usual plantations, it occurred to me that we humans consume an awful lot of sugar and bananas. The beach was nice yellow sand, and the adjacent caravan park was packed to the rafters. I did my usual evening scratch around for a campsite and scraped one out on the roadside near the transfer station. It was quiet. The mosquitoes here were in appalling numbers and the fornicating little fornicators could only be countered by covering up as much as possible and, yet again, with the liberal application of chemicals to even the tiniest area of exposed skin.

Day 24

I did a four-kilometre walk along the beach the following morning, which I find is a good start to any but the most miserable of weather days. Bramston Beach is quite steep, which made the walk a bit harder on my ageing ankles, but to make up for it I had the place virtually to myself. I met only one couple and their very excitable six-month-old Labrador, Olly.

I stopped only briefly at Innisfail, mainly to go to the chemist, then, as I continued south on the Bruce and on entering the town of El Arish, I happened to see the turn-off to Mission Beach and decided to take it. I had heard good things about the place so, as per the usual *modus operandi* for this trip, on a whim I decided to have a look. Such whims give you a sense of freedom which is, in itself, perhaps the most important ingredient of utopia.

The name, El Arish, piqued my interest and I immediately suspected a connection to one of the world wars. The Egyptian city after which it is named is located in Sinai on the Mediterranean coast. A quick check of the Australian War Memorial site didn't provide much information about the place other than that it was occupied by the Turks and taken by British forces on 21 December 1916. Another site mentions that this force included the Australian Light Horse. It was then used as an important base from which further operations emanated. The Queensland town was founded in 1921 to serve as the hub of a soldier-settlement area. Many of its streets are named after high-ranking officers such as Monash and Chauvel.

Driving towards Mission Beach, I travelled through what were becoming familiar surrounds. The sugar cane and banana orchards of the flat country give way to lush green hills and cattle nearer to the coast and then, finally, the rainforest strip along the coast. I took the drive to Bingil Bay, which struck me as a pretty and very green little place probably choked with alternative lifestylers. Mission Beach was sunny, warm, and busy. I liked the feel of the place straight away so I decided to stay for a couple of nights. It wasn't as big as I expected it to be; it had more of a village feel. The pub looked good, there were a few bars and eateries, not too many shops and, most importantly, there was a fish and chip shop.

The first caravan park was full but, fortunately for me, the second one had a few unpowered sites right at the back far right corner, which suited me just fine because there was shade from the adjacent forest. So, with some time to relax at Mission Beach, having a shower and washing some clothes and bedding and having a spell from driving, I felt very content. My good humour improved further with my unexpected encounter with another Ulysses butterfly, in the caravan park of all places. Their blue is so striking that it is hard to believe they are real and yet there it was, fluttering about for a while as if to show itself off for my benefit and privilege, until our lives diverged.

After hot chips and a piece of fish, I could think of nothing better than to do a long walk. If this is beginning to sound somewhat repetitive, then it surely was, apologies for that, but the evening was calm and balmy and the beach was most inviting. It was very flat and incredibly wide, perhaps close to a hundred metres across at the low point of the tide. The walking path through the forest beside the beach was every bit as alluring so I did a long loop using both the beach and the path.

The ever present south-easterly seemed to have paused for a breather. There were a few people on the beach but not many and still no-one swam. I was clean, refreshed, full, working the legs, gazing out to sea and at coconut palms and into people's backyards, and I just felt bloody good. I much preferred Mission Beach to Port Douglas and Palm Cove. It was more my style.

From the beach, one can see Dunk Island and, further to the south, the craggy tops of Hinchinbrook.

Mission Beach,
You are a peach.
No need for cream,
Just to dream.
Mission impossible?
Nay, mission accomplished.

Day 25

Day twenty-five was a day of rest, reading and beach walking. One occurrence stood out, as I sat on the throne doing the disagreeable thing that one must do on a regular basis. I heard a man at the urinal and then another man enter the toilet block. Said one to the other, 'We meet again,' to which the other replied, 'We must have the same size bladder.' I smiled to myself.

Day 26

I hit the road early on the following day. After the debacle of Mossman Gorge, I decided to give Tully Gorge a miss. There were too many big and fancy signs with photos on them for my liking. I also gave Murray Falls the back of my head; the truth is, and I know this may sound ungrateful, that I was waterfalled out. I decided that I would go to Wallaman Falls, however, as it is so high, but that would be the last for this trip.

I stopped at Cardwell and stared across the sea to Hinchinbrook for a while before moving on to Ingham, where I had the good fortune of visiting the botanic garden. The garden is quite drab but, with my Italian heritage, I was most pleasantly surprised to find there a memorial to the Alpini. This famous regiment fought in the mountains during both world wars and the men proudly wore a very distinctive hat, the Capello Alpino, with its single raven feather at the back. I quote from the memorial:

> Who were the Alpini?
>
> The elite Italian mountain troop regiment, the Alpini, was established in 1872. It served with distinction in the largely unheralded but bloody three-year campaign, 1915–1918, in the mountains between Italy and Austria against elite units of the Austro-Hungarian Empire and Germany. This campaign became known by its combatants as the 'War in Snow and Ice.' The Alpini is the oldest mountain infantry regiment in the world and is internationally recognised as one of the world's elite military units. It served with distinction in Afghanistan with its NATO allies in the war against terror.
>
> Post-war, many of these soldiers migrated to Australia and settled

in the Ingham area to work on the sugar cane plantations. However, the first boatload of Italians to arrive in Queensland to work in the sugar industry was way back in 1891 aboard the ship *Junma*.

The memorial consists of a single column atop which sits the eagle, the symbol of the Alpini. Just below is a bronze replica of the hat and adjacent are two flagpoles, bearing the Australian and Italian flags. It is a touching tribute to those brave souls and made me proud of my Italian heritage. So often mocked the world over for cowardice during the world wars, up there, in the mountains, they fought bravely against the Austrians, who generally held the high ground. Italian forces were almost always poorly trained, poorly led, and provided with second-rate arms, leading to defeats and low morale.

As luck would have it, after a brief walk around the garden, I happened to wander into the plant conservatory to find one of the council workers in there doing a great job of tidying the place up: weeding, mulching and planting. We discussed plants for a while; in particular, some of the fine specimens of orchids in the place. She was also able to identify a tree I had seen a great deal of in my travels. Its mass of vivid red flowers seemed to pop up everywhere and was a frequent delight but, alas, it is a weed; it is the African tulip tree.

After a bit more plant talk, I left her to her work and made for the Tyto Wetlands, which is also in Ingham, where I did a four-kilometre walk and had the good fortune of seeing a red-backed fairy wren for the first time in my life. I wouldn't want you to get the impression that glimpsing a red-backed fairy wren was a momentous life-changing event but it was pretty special all the same.

As I alluded to earlier, the thought of visiting another waterfall did not exactly thrill me. The feeling reminded me of the trip I did to Italy, a long time ago. It was the same feeling I would get before visiting yet another church or one more art gallery, which seem to be on every street corner in that country. I was getting bored with toppling water and I don't handle being bored very well. There are a finite number of times that I can stare at plunging water before I begin to get restless, but Wallaman Falls is Wallaman Falls and you cannot just drive on past it; at least, I cannot. You see, it is the highest permanent single-drop waterfall in Australia, which makes it rather compelling.

The drive to the falls is gorgeous, passing through farmland and then into refreshingly cool rainforest. It is a very short walk from the car park to the falls lookout and I stared at the falls for a good while, from both vantage points, both being well barricaded. It freefalls for 269 metres into a pool that is twenty metres deep. Access to the top of the falls is closed but there is a track that takes you to the bottom, but I was tired and it was getting late so, despite the considerable pangs of guilt that disturb me whenever I encounter a walking track that I ignore, I didn't take it.

I returned to the Bruce and decided to camp at or near Lucinda, as I wanted to see the famous jetty. This monolith is almost six kilometres long and is used to load sugar onto large ships out in deep water. It is worth seeing, particularly with Hinchinbrook Island in the background.

I stayed the night at a small clearing at the 'Welcome to Lucinda' sign, unaware that I was mostly surrounded by swamps. I had the pleasure of mosquitoes and midges for company as well as the soothing rattle of sugar trains going to and fro for most of the night.

Day 27

After a very average sleep, the following day, day twenty-seven, was a quiet one. I bypassed Townsville, went on to Ayr and, once more, on a whim, turned off; this time to Alva Beach.

The town of Alva Beach is nice, quiet, with a few houses and a shaded picnic area on the foreshore. The beach itself and the adjacent dunes are awesome. You can walk to the beach, of course, but there is also a vehicular track wending its way through the soft sands of the dunes to the beach and it was along that track that I found a perfect campsite in the shade of a large pandanus and an equally large acacia.

Apart from the blustery south-easterly whipping up sand, it was good to walk along the beach and dunes and to look out at the extensive sandbars. The place is renowned as a turtle hatchery, where the mothers come to bury their eggs in the sand from October to March. I know that because there were signs saying so. What I didn't know, and what there were no signs telling me, is that the place is also renowned for sandflies that like to bury their chompers into skin, any skin, my skin.

Day 28

It was not until the following morning that I was made aware of the fact that I was in sandfly territory, as my lower legs were covered in at least two score bites. I react badly to sandfly bites and their intense itch was making a cretin out of me. I hate the little shits, I have a phobia of them, the knowledge of their presence induces in me a panic which breaks all moorings with reason, resulting in a compulsion to cover up and douse myself with chemicals if I must cohabitate with them or, preferably, clear the hell out.

I cleared out, quick smart, and just as quickly developed a healthy dose of self-preserving paranoia about the bloodsuckers. I was pissed off with myself for letting my guard down; I was determined that it would not happen again.

I bypassed Bowen and made straight for Airley Beach, the, well, I'm sure you already know, gateway to the Whitsundays. I had heard of the place, I wanted to see it and then I wanted to leave. *Veni, vidi, ire.* I am sure that most of you by now could have predicted my reaction to the place; I didn't like it. Far too developed, far too touristy, far too commercial, and far too many shops, eateries and boozeries for my liking; and the beach isn't even that good. It was overcast and drizzling, which did not help, but still, it was far too hectic for me. The streets were full of people and the marina was full of boats and there was even an ocean liner parked out to sea. Welcome to the gateway to the Whitsundays.

I walked around the gateway to hell for a bit and then left.

That night, the search for a campsite was a particularly desperate one. There was nothing by the roadside except sugar cane plantations, everywhere, which left scant land for anything else. Finally, and as an immense relief to my growing consternation, I borrowed a great piece of what I was certain was private land between a lagoon and a field of sugarcane somewhere south of Proserpine and just a short way along the Lethebrook road. I just hoped that an angry gun-toting farmer wouldn't find me. I felt pretty safe on a dirt road, hidden between the bush and trees of the lagoon and the screen of the cane and invisible from the main road I had turned off to get here. It was a great find as long as a farmer's feathers remained unruffled. I celebrated my discovery by tasting sugar cane juice for the first time in my life and, yep, it was sweet.

The lagoon was beautiful; its tranquil water soothing and, for the first time this trip, I felt like dangling a line but I didn't have one. There was a pair of large birds, I think they were kites, nesting in a large tree on the opposite bank, then, as the sun set and the lagoon shone like a jewel and the trees seemed to come alive simply through the force of vibrant colour, a flock of ibis arrived to roost for the night, also in the trees opposite.

I was entertained by their antics as they settled down for the night. I deduced that ibis come in two forms – one that makes up its mind, chooses a branch on which to perch and sticks with it; the other, a querulous, envious and indecisive variety, is never satisfied with its own and will always see a branch on which another of its comrades is perched as superior in a way which, I have to confess, remained obscure to me throughout. The latter variety hops, skips, jumps and flaps from branch to branch, creating general mayhem in the process, unsettling those who have just settled and causing much raucous trouble and invective. They create a disturbance of the peace that often results in the peace-loving variety having to move on to find peace, often of the temporary sort, elsewhere. Not so unlike us lot, really, when you think about it. I think I fell asleep long before they all did only to be woken by more of their carryings-on with the coming of dawn.

Day 29

I was breakfasting when a ute came along and stopped alongside mine. I braced myself for an angry farmer to emerge from the vehicle to vent his spleen on me but I am happy to report that his spleen stayed put, tucked right up there, unvented, in his left upper quadrant. He was a very decent chap.

It turned out that the farmer, Peter, wasn't averse to campers but he was wary of them because some had unintentionally set fire to the adjacent cane plantation in the past. I was already in bed, listening to the ibis, when he came past the previous evening, walking his dog, to suss me out. Not seeing a campfire, and seeing the Cookies (Cooktown orchids) and the ginger plant I had put out to get some fresh air, he decided that I must be OK and moved on.

We must have talked for about an hour and a half. He did most of the talking and I did most of the listening, which is usually the way with me. His father was a cane-grower and I think his grandfather as well so, needless to say, he was a mine of information about the sugar industry. He told me about the hard old days of cutting cane by hand, burning the fields, near misses with snakes and a disease the cane-cutters were prone to known as Weil's disease or leptospirosis, a bacterial disease caught from contact with infected rat's urine.

He spoke about the modern, mechanised process for growing and harvesting the cane and what is done with it but sometimes he still liked to cut a little by hand. Then he mentioned something fascinating: a neighbour of his called John who has a pet crocodile called Charlene.

Charlene is a local celebrity. Once, when she was smaller and society was less regulated, she would go into town with the family and even go into the local pub and sit at the bar, but then she grew up and nowadays she must remain in a strong enclosure. Once, she bit part of John's father's hand off thinking that it was a fish! John's father blamed his own stupidity for the mishap but it seems that pet crocodiles can't tell the difference between fish and the hand that feeds them, which is a bit of a worry. I suppose they are either dumb, have very poor eyesight or simply do not care; either way, I would not recommend getting too close.

In a classic 'every dog has its day' moment, John's father became a bit of a celebrity for a while as a real-life Crocodile Dundee during the period of that movie's fame and he and his wife were taken on an all-expenses paid trip to the US by some enterprising film crew where he spent a fair bit of time swanning around dressed like Crocodile Dundee. Why not? Good luck to him. I hope he got a buck or two out of it.

Then we got onto the disaster of cane toads. Originally from south and central America, the cane toad was brought to Australia from Hawaii in 1935 in an attempt to control cane beetle, the larvae of which grow underground, feeding on the sugar cane roots, thus killing or reducing the vigour of the plant and greatly reducing yields.

In an era well before environment impact studies were a serious thing, someone who hadn't done any research at all or perhaps had done a little, badly, decided that letting them in would be a good idea. That person had learnt nothing from the introduction of rabbits, foxes, cats et cetera into Australia. Perhaps while sitting in a bar in Honolulu, downing some beers with some of the locals, he must have heard one of the pickled Hawaiians, who'd in all probability never been within cooee of sugar cane, sing the praises of this ugly, voracious and poisonous reptile as some sort of cane beetle exterminator. Maybe in Hawaii they are but here, according to Peter, they found much better things to feed on as they don't particularly like feeding on our hard-shelled cane beetles and they can't get at the larvae because they are underground!

If you are scratching your head at this moment, then you are not alone. Since the toad's introduction to the Gordonvale region, it has marched relentlessly right across northern Australia, feeding on native animals and, because of its poison glands, killing anything that feeds on it. It was a smart move bringing it here. An act of pure genius. Its introduction has been a complete disaster to our native fauna and the cane toad has no redeeming features whatsoever. It is reviled and yet it is blameless. I hope that the person responsible had some cane toads shoved down his/her throat and up his/her arse.

A couple of final things about cane toads before moving on. Little gems provided by Peter. Golf clubs are still used, apparently, plus, another thing I was completely unaware of, which is that people consume small quantities of their poison as a hallucinogen! Some people! Seriously?

By the end of our chat, I happened to mention that I was retired and Peter offered me a job driving cane trucks; start right away, no experience necessary. I declined, but not without a brief 'what if' moment. But Port Albert is home and Melbourne is family.

I stopped at Sarina Beach for lunch and to stretch the legs but my burning legs pushed my terror of sandflies to new heights, so I didn't linger on the nice sandy beaches. A fast walk in the shallows and a speed-walk to the gorgeous Johnson Beach and back was all I dared risk. You can't swim in the sea because of crocs and you can't linger on the sand because of sandflies, so I began to wonder what was the point of going to all these beaches, beautiful as they are. It was all getting rather exasperating so you will understand why I decided to head inland, where there are only mossies and midges to deal with. I took the back road from Sarina to Marlborough for a change of scenery and the absence of beaches.

I had the usual trouble finding a place to camp for the night. Everywhere was private property and fences. Eventually, I found a sizeable clearing by the side of the road, near the Clermont turn-off and a railway line. I had a reasonable sleep despite some traffic noise and the occasional train.

Day 30

The morning of day thirty was foggy, cool, and damp. It made for unpleasant camping but pleasant driving, apart from the incessant roadworks, as I continued to Marlborough, cruising on eighty, with the road virtually to myself. It was hilly cattle country.

I stopped at Marlborough for a rest but only briefly, as I saw nothing that interested me much.

I broke the law that night in my choice of campsite. I visited Mt Etna National Park (yes, further proof of Roman occupation of Australia for all you doubting Thomases), near the Caves, and, being thoroughly sick of scratching around for one all the time, I decided to stop there for the night, just like that, without a booking, without a permit and without handing over a zac to anybody. The place was dead. There were only a couple of other visitors for the entire afternoon and they didn't hang about. I felt quite confident that the Gestapo wouldn't find me and drag me away for questioning.

It is a small national park, much of it is scrappy weed-filled rehabilitated land but it has an interesting history to do with caves, bats, cement and people with different points of view. It was the sight of a prolonged environmental battle with the usual themes between the usual antagonists. On one side, the mining industry and jobs, specifically, the mining of limestone to make cement. On the other side, the Greenies, the pejorative moniker for the much-despised people who want to preserve what little that is left of those special natural places that have not already been destroyed by human activity in this country. In this case, the environmentalists wanted to save the limestone caves and their bat population.

Many people don't care about bats but some do. The Bat Battle of

Mt Etna became Queensland's longest-running conservation conflict, beginning in 1966 and ending in 1999. It was heated and at times hostile and it divided locals, friends and families.

The caves had been mined before, to extract bat guano for fertiliser. Then, in the early 1960s, Central Queensland Cement, CQC, took out mining leases on and around Mt Etna to exploit the large limestone deposits. Mining began around 1965 and the first shots in the war came soon after from local cavers and the University of Queensland Speleological Society, UQSS, who expressed concerns about the impact of mining on the caves and their bats.

In 1966, when the beautiful Resurrection Cave was found to have been damaged by blasting, complaints were made to the Rockhampton mayor and a public meeting was held the following year and concerned locals united to form the Central Queensland Speleological Society, CQSS.

The battle between CQC and conservationists raged until 1990. Caves were damaged and bats were killed. Queensland needed cement. Miners did not want to lose their jobs over some bats that they thought could simply go and live somewhere else. They were the issues. Legal action was instigated to stop mining in some areas to protect caves and bats. Conservationists organised cave tours to raise public awareness, trespassed onto leased land to occupy the caves and prevent further blasting and, somewhat ironically, filled in drill holes with cement.

The Queensland government of the time largely supported the mining industry, therefore real change did not take effect until there was a change of government and environmental issues became more important to Queenslanders and to Australians as a whole. All mining on Mt Etna finally ceased in 2004 then, in 2008, Cement Australia handed over the former mine site of CQC for inclusion in the Mt Etna National Park. Like all places where the land has been disturbed, weeds take over, but nature itself, and people, are gradually fixing the damaged mountain and the bats now mostly live in peace.

The issue raised once more a fundamental issue: does Earth exist to merely serve the dominant species or do other species have just as much right to their piece of this planet and a right to live on it unmolested? That debate, I'm afraid, is way beyond the parameters of this work but it is one that is taken much more seriously than in the past.

Day 31

The following day, I went to Yeppoon. I had been there before, way back in my student days, forty years ago. I remembered very little about the place but I was curious to see it again. I remembered Great Keppel Island better, going there twice with some colleagues from Rockhampton. I also remembered the tourism ads for Great Keppel as a great place to get wrecked and, while I didn't exactly get wrecked there either time, I did get mildly demolished. It was a fun place where I learned to sailboard and I subsequently bought one with my first decent pay packet and I still have it to this day, although it now sits around, completely idle, serving merely as a nostalgic memento of my youth.

I didn't think much of Yeppoon. To me, it lacked soul. It seemed to be more to do with real estate than anything else. I did notice that Matthew Flinders seems to feature prominently in the area, as he often does in other parts of this country, but I don't know the connection he had with the Yeppoon area.

I enjoyed the drive south along the coast to Emu Park. It reminded me of a short version of the Great Ocean Road in Victoria. Emu Park is a little ripper of a place. I loved it. In fact, I loved it so much that I decided to stay for a couple of nights as I was due for a shower, some clothes needed to be washed and I wanted a break from driving. Emu Park suited me down to the ground and up to the air but unfortunately, and not in any way surprisingly, the caravan park was full so I had to settle for a site at another caravan park about five kilometres out of the town.

Emu Park had everything I need: the right size, not overdeveloped, a nice beach, some parkland, a pub, fish and chips, and a supermarket. It also happened to have one of the best Anzac memorials I have ever seen and the impressive *Singing Ship* sculpture.

I had walked the beach at Yeppoon in the morning and the beach at Emu Park in the afternoon and, finally, the beach opposite the caravan park where I was staying, in the evening. I enjoy walking, it helps to keep me physically fit and mentally better, but the monotony of all these beach walks was beginning to do my head in. If you recall what I said about churches and art galleries in Italy, and, earlier on this trip, about waterfalls, I now felt exactly the same way about beaches. I was getting bored to death with them but they were somewhere to walk, often when there was nowhere else.

In what amounted to an embarrassingly puerile dummy spit, I refused to take any more beach photos that evening. In fact, in an act of protest, I photographed anything but the beach: bus stops, bus stop signs, wheely bins, weird letterboxes, witch's hats in people's gardens, coconuts on the ground, art gallery signs and other oddities. I posted them on Facebook and that act somehow seemed to allay, in part at least, my fed-up state. Bizarre, I know. I think some of my friends were getting a little worried. But it's just me and my odd ways.

Day 32

So what did I do the following morning? I went on a five-kilometre beach walk, of course. What else was there? It was either that or walking on the road and I didn't fancy the road; besides, a beach is nice early in the morning before the wind picks up. Many of the beaches I've seen up this way are sandy mudflats and very wide at low tide which makes for easy walking but what I really fancied, as the day heated up, was a swim. Fortunately, the caravan park had a good pool but the water was chilling and I couldn't stay in for long. I spent the rest of the afternoon lounging in the shade and reading *Vanity Fair*, a deliciously satirical book that I enjoyed immensely.

To get the best photos, I had decided to wait until the light of evening to visit the Anzac Memorial and the *Singing Ship*. I would travel a long way to see them at any time of the day but the going down of the sun made it much more poignant.

Much of the memorial consists of cut sandstone blocks, which came alive with the mellow evening glow, arranged so as to form a court, the Anzac Court. In the centre are five sandstone pillars representing each of the five Australian infantry divisions that fought in World War I.

The backdrop to the court is an extraordinary pictorial screen sculpture, a representation in metal of Frank Hurley's famous photograph taken near Hodge, Belgium, on 5 October 1917. It portrays sixteen soldiers of the 1st Australian Infantry Division walking on duckboards above a water-filled bomb crater. In the photograph, they are clearly visible on the skyline and their reflections can clearly be seen in the water below. Some minor changes from the original photo were made to two of the soldiers. The eighth soldier's head was turned to look back and his hand is outstretched as if to give aid. The ninth soldier's gear on his back has the appearance of angel's wings and his bayonet looks like a Christian cross. It is a wonderful sculpture of a very moving photo, knowing what they were heading for. Well done to all who were responsible for its creation.

There are two flagpoles, flying the Australian and New Zealand flags, and adjacent to the memorial is a grassed earth mound which 'is intended to evoke the sacred nature of earth and its associations with burial'.

The Memorial Walk isn't long and is nothing like the path those brave sixteen had to take to relieve their comrades on the front line. It leads from Anzac Court through a well maintained garden. It takes you to an enclosure that is stuffed full of information about World War I and there are signs along the way covering specific aspects such as the controversy over who actually shot down Manfred von Richthofen, otherwise known as the Red Baron: a British or Canadian fighter pilot or an Australian shooting from the ground. I am sure that each country would like to claim the credit but from what I have gleaned, the weight of evidence seems to favour the Australian. Either way, the German fighter ace with the most confirmed kills of World War I was buried with full military honours by his enemy, as a mark of respect and a reminder that war is not always confined to hatred and savagery.

Along the Memorial Walk there is also an outstanding representation of a painting, on transparent glass. The original painting, *The Spirit-Gallipoli Landing 1915*, is a work by a British military painter, David Rowlands. It 'depicts the second wave of the 10th battalion (South Australia) scaling banks of Anzac Cove at 5 a.m. This was 30 minutes after the initial landing by parts of the 9th (Queensland), 10th and the 11th (Western Australia).' The representation on glass enables one to look at the work and to see through it to Keppel Bay in the background, creating a scene that, with a little imagination, could be Anzac Cove. It is very well done.

Beyond the enclosure are three forests of posts in the ground with each forest representing one of the armed services, and each post is inscribed with the name of an engagement in which the service fought.

Finally, at the top of the rise, the walk ends at the *Singing Ship*. This remarkable sculpture resembles a very large harp with three tensioned cables which produce a beautiful musical resonance when moving air is applied to them. The plaque on the sculpture 'honours Captain James Cook, 1728—1779, explorer, navigator, cartographer who discovered and named Keppel Bay, 26–28th May 1770.'

Everything about the place was most impressive and it is a fine tribute to the Anzacs, to Cook and to the hard work of the people of the town, which is only a small town, who made it happen. Well done to you all.

All that remained after such an emotional experience was to have a beer at the pub and think of what the fallen and those that survived went through, in all conflicts.

I felt some regret at leaving Emu Park the next day. I had fallen in love with the place, almost as much as I had fallen for Cooktown. It was a big gem in a small jewellery box and, just like finding any gem, it came as a most pleasant surprise. Still, the show had to go on and I found myself becoming somewhat homesick. I was missing my plants, all the dogs I knew and, before you conclude that I am a total misanthrope, for I am not, only a partial one, even some of the people.

Day 33

Day thirty-three began once more with fog. Two things of note happened today: I left the tropics and disaster was averted.

I had planned to stop at Rockhampton Hospital, where I had spent some time as a final-year medical student, but the tide of peak-hour traffic was too much to fight against and there were too many traffic lights for my liking so I got out of Rocky as fast as the traffic would allow.

I turned off to Calliope to do the right thing by a friend of mine whose son had recently bought a house there. She guided me to the joint over the phone and, yep, it did indeed look like a house. Anyway, duty done, I hung up and hit the road again. I also had a brief look at a large and rustic, free campground on the banks of the Calliope River, off the old Bruce Highway. The old ford is now closed off by a barrier so it is only possible to get there via the southern approach. I decided not to stay as it was too early in the day and it was nothing special, other than being free.

I planned to stay the night somewhere around 1770 or Agnes Waters but the access road was cut by a bad accident and the word travelling down the banked-up line of cars was that it would take a while to reopen, so I immediately joined the throng doing U-turns and retraced my way back to the Bruce at Miriam Vale.

I stopped for a rest at Gin Gin. I happened upon a sign there proclaiming that in some year or other it had been Queensland's friendliest town. I chuckled to myself over that one. I wondered how the hell these things are decided and by whom; some committee, I suppose. Anyway, it has clearly gone down the gurgler from whatever year it was judged worthy of such an award because, while I was there at any rate, I wasn't accosted by a single beaming face, nor was I offered a free beer or even a glass of water by a living soul. It seemed to me to be your run-of-the-mill average friendly, not especially friendly, town and I could scarce believe that it would be in the running for this year's award.

I had heard from quite a few people of the beauty of Elliot Heads but getting there meant going through Bundaberg and, as you may have already deduced, I am averse to big-town traffic, so, figuring that one head would be pretty much as good as any other, I decided to go to Burrum Heads instead. When I finally arrived, it provided a sanctuary from the crazy amount of roadworks between Calliope and Howard that was seriously affecting my sanity. I don't know if any of you have groaned out loud to yourself when yet another yellow sign has appeared round the next bend, a mere two minutes after leaving behind the last batch. I know it has to be done, all that roadwork, I get that, but does it all have to be done when I'm around? Poor planning. Someone must be held to account and top decks must roll.

Burrum Heads was yet another small, picturesque Queensland coastal town, with an estuary, a beach and some boats. The caravan park looked packed and, besides, I wanted somewhere more sheltered from the wind that was brisk and bracing so I decided to break the law again, find shelter from the wind in the arms of loving boughs and try to find somewhere to stop in the Burrum Coast National Park.

As usual, eking out a spot in the bush to camp was easier thought than done. I drove quite a way but the bush was thick and no clearing whatsoever presented itself. I kept going, deeper and deeper into the national park, expecting any moment to come upon the Burrum River but, as the road became narrower and the thick bush on either side created the effect of a tunnel, suddenly appearing in front of me was not a river but an impenetrable swamp.

I broke hard and managed to avoid going into the water. That was the easy part; turning around was going to be the problem. The Cruiser's turning circle is about the size of the MCG and there was very little room to manoeuvre on either side of the road and reversing any distance would be a nightmare, so I guessed at having to do an eleven-point turn to extricate myself.

On the first attempt, the rear wheels got bogged in the mushy edge of the track and, with the weight of the girl, she wasn't budging even in low-ratio four-wheel drive. I'd learned long ago of the futility of spinning the wheels in wet bog; all you do is go deeper and deeper into the mire and the resulting effort required to get out increases exponentially.

I got out of the car. I didn't panic. I assessed the situation. All four wheels had spun in the mud and had turned into slicks but the rear wheels were not in too deep and the front wheels hardly at all. That was good news. Another piece of good news was that mine was evidently not the first car to get into strife here. There was a tiny area on the opposite side of the road that had been cleared of scrub, albeit rather rudimentarily, to enable a turnaround. It was also drier there so, if I could just get my partner unstuck, I should be able to turn round but with some difficulty.

Not getting myself out of this pickle would be a giant pain in a big fat arse I didn't want to think about. The best chance was to get it right the first time, so I prepared meticulously. With a trowel, I dug the wheels out of the mud as much as I could and laid branches under them. I cleared some of the branches opposite to give myself more room to turn around and so the partner wouldn't get scratched to pieces. Once everything was in readiness to my satisfaction, I got back in the car, feeling a bit anxious, started her up, put her in gear, and out she came, quite easily. A nine-point turn later and I was leaving the swamp behind, feeling very much relieved.

Shortly after, I found a dull little clearing at a road intersection where I could spend the night. It was a long time since I cared about the dullness of a place to camp; just flattish and clear enough to fit me and my car was ample. Just about anything would do, even adjacent to a tip or a piggery would have sufficed on this particular night as it was getting late, finding anywhere suitable was nigh on impossible, and the residual euphoria which I clung to at my successful extraction from the swamp made it impossible for me to be daunted and aesthetic pleasures completely unnecessary.

Nearby was a farm and on its fence was a sign that said something like 'If you are bogged we can't help, phone Derm' and there was Derm's phone number next to his name. It must be a nice little earner for Derm but, unfortunately for him, his services were not needed this day.

Day 34

Day thirty-four was cold, grey and drizzly all day, but the days ahead looked promising, which gave me a green light for Fraser Island. The prospect greatly excited me. Incidentally, the island was named after Eliza Fraser, who was shipwrecked on the island with her husband, Captain James Fraser, in 1836. The original Aboriginal name for the island is K'gari, apparently pronounced 'Gurri', which means paradise in the language of the original inhabitants, the Butchulla people. The name was recently officially changed to K'gari by the Queensland government so I will use that name.

Harvey Bay is a hole. I stopped there for essentials, then went straight on to River Heads and booked myself a spot on the three thirty ferry to Kingfisher Bay. It was $212 return and the trip takes around forty-five minutes. The rest of the day was spent stuffing around online, getting permits. Camping was seven dollars per night per person and then there was the island driving permit, which was $55 per month.

The budget took a hit but I wasn't just going anywhere, I was going to K'gari, and fulfilling a long-term dream and finally consigning my envy for people who had been there and raved on about how good it is to where envy belongs.

I decided to go for four nights but, having done bugger-all research, I agonised for some time over where to stay. There are so many campsites; I had no idea there were that many. In the end, as is my wont, I opted for keeping it simple and booked all four nights at Central Station.

I knew that four nights would not give me enough time to see the entire island, not properly at least, and I certainly did not want to rush around trying to cram in as much as I could by driving around on sand the whole time. I wanted to do more walking and less driving. Central station, most aptly named, provided a central location from which to explore the southern half of the island. It has walking tracks, it is set amongst thick forest and is far more sheltered from the wind, it has good facilities and plenty of campsites and is adjacent to rainforest. It sounded ideal, and it was.

I had to get a move on if I was to get to Central Station before dark, so I didn't linger at the Kingfisher Bay Resort. I let my tyres down to twenty psi at the servo there and hit the sandy road. Driving on the sand roads of K'gari for the first time was exciting and fun but it is slow going, which would be far from a problem normally but on this occasion, I was racing against the setting sun. You definitely need high clearance on your vehicle; I saw one car get stuck in soft deep sand and have to be towed out. And one must constantly be on the lookout for oncoming traffic as the roads are narrow and one or both vehicles have to pull to the side of the road to get through. You wouldn't want to have to do it every day to get to your nine-to-five job, but on holiday, and with the novelty of it, it was an experience.

I arrived at Central Station just on dusk. What I could see of the place and the tall, darkened trees looked impressive, like straight, towering columns. I very much looked forward to seeing it the following day, with the benefit of daylight.

> Say nothing when words can only fail.
> Write nothing when justice cannot be done to the tale.
> Rather, simply walk along Wanggoolba Creek,
> A place the nature lover should seek.

I am not usually fickle and I try not to be hypocritical, of the do as I say and not as I do variety, but I will be now. By all means, walk along Wanggoolba Creek. I did and you would be mad not to. Speak if you must. If your oratory is Shakespearean, you just might do the place justice, but I will not speak. I will, however, contravene the second line of verse that I have just written! How dare I? Such arrogance! I will do my best to put K'gari into prose. It cannot possibly come up to the mark, it will inevitably fail, but I shall give it my best shot.

Day 35

I awoke next morning to a visual feast. The grey, the cold, the drizzle, had been swept away by a mysticism that seems so congruous with the natural shrine that is K'gari. My eyes breakfasted hungrily on this superb campground set amongst imposing kauri pine, hoop pine and satinay. It was sensual gluttony of the first order that made me hungry for more. I watched the straight trunks soar to the sky, I touched the rough bark of the hoop and the scaly plaques of the kauri and I smelt their faint odour of pine resin. The car keys did not leave my pocket. I wanted to walk every track and savour as much as I could from the island's sumptuous menu.

First, I wanted to see Wanggoolba Creek, as it is close to the campground, basically running beside its eastern edge. It can be done as a short loop of 700 metres or a longer loop of four kilometres by taking in Pile Valley, the headwaters of the creek. I chose the latter, but first, nature was calling, and it was while sitting on the throne that I spotted a fine piece of scripture. Most toilet graffiti is pretty lame, puerile stuff almost always of a banal sexual nature, but here I found an exceptional piece that made me chuckle as I sat there and even feel a little smug.

On the wall, someone possessing extraordinary insight penned some words about different makes of car and the typical person who drives them. I'm not sure how much science was behind it but anecdotally it was on solid ground methinks. Unfortunately, I couldn't make out what it said about Ranger drivers. Perhaps one such driver had erased it, which would be typical. I have my own opinion on Ranger drivers which I will not divulge as it may put my life at risk. Suffice to say that your average Ranger driver would use books solely as fire-starters and I am surprised that one was able to read the graffiti and actually comprehend it sufficiently to want to censor it. But I am making far too many assumptions so I will move on before I get into real trouble.

It went on, 'Land Rover = light skin + sandles [sic]'. No argument from me on that one. 'Jeep = brain dead'. Say no more. And finally, 'Toyota = smart, easy going'. Modesty forbids me from taking the ultimate observation any further, other than to say that I agree wholeheartedly. Clearly, it was written by a true intellect.

Having dealt with matters that could not be deferred, I proceeded to the creek. At first glance, I thought that the creek was polluted and felt astonished that this could be so. It seemed an impossibility and yet my eyes were not deceiving me. There was a definite milky colouring to the creek. As I got closer, however, I realised that it was the creek that was deceiving me and what I was seeing was the creek bottom, which consisted of pure white sand seen through perfectly clear water. The effect was remarkable as the presence of the untarnished water is made evident solely by silent ripples and the reflections of stream-side vegetation.

Kauri pine, tall piccabeen palms, tree ferns and king ferns lined the banks of the creek. Mosses abounded. I was stunned by the new pink growth on the syzygium and the ostentatious presence of vivid red fungi. It was good to see my friends, the king ferns, *Angiopteris evecta*, with their incredibly long fronds, again. I had last seen them in a tiny remnant cluster at Carnarvon Gorge but here, in this moist and sheltered gully, they were more numerous and seemed much less vulnerable despite it being the only spot on the island where they are to be found. A remarkable fact is that its massive fronds lack woody tissue to support them; rather, they rely on the pressure of water, like water in a hose or, if you'll pardon the analogy, erectile tissue. Nature really is amazing.

The piccabeen, or bangalow, palms thrive on the banks of the creek, reaching impressive heights. Aborigines used the fronds for basket weaving and the sheath at the base of the fronds as a coolamon (carrying bowl).

Part of the creek walk is on a raised wooden walkway which makes for pleasant strolling in the cool, still gully. At one point, it has a sculpture made by a German woman, Monika Bayer, featuring three wooden posts each with a separate title. *Rainforest Relicts* (sic) has what appears to me to be palm and fern fronds carved into it. *Sounds of life, listen to the locals* has, somewhat oddly given the title, the body and head of a snake. *Strangler fig* features an ornate carving of a strangler fig. The sculpture looks good and fits in with the environment perfectly.

The Pile Valley section of the walk was once heavily logged for satinay or Fraser Island turpentine, *Syncarpia hillii*. The tree is easily distinguished by the deeply furrowed bark on its tall straight trunk. The wood was used for heavy construction as well as furniture, including furnishings for the old Parliament House in Canberra and the then prime minister's cottage. The resistance of its timber to marine borer made it also suitable for the construction of docks and jetties, some of it even being used in the London docks and the Suez Canal. Nowadays, it is hard to believe that a place of such beauty could have been logged and also mined for sand, but that was the way of the past and the only way to change that was with yet another conservation battle.

Personally, my soul wishes that humanity did not have to mine or log at all but my head understands that it is simply not possible if we seek to maintain the way of life we have achieved. At this very moment, I am using a lot of timber and the products of mining to build a house. So it goes on, but places like K'gari should never be exploited in that way and thanks to those who fought to save it, it is now almost entirely protected as a national park which was proclaimed a World Heritage Area in 1992. The flora and fauna must be pleased for they flourish and it was a great delight to have a chilled goanna calmly saunter through my campsite one morning.

Logging began in 1863 and from 1920, Central Station was the centre of logging operations. Timber workers lived there and it had a garage/workshop, stables and even a school. All logging ceased on K'gari in 1991.

Sand mining on K'gari began in 1949 and ceased in 1976 after conservationists took the case to the High Court of Australia.

Day 36

My second day on K'gari was spent discovering some of the southern lakes; Birrabeen, Benardon and Boomanjin, via the southern lakes scenic drive. For me, the novelty of driving on sand evaporated very quickly. One sees so much more when walking.

The inland lakes on K'gari are perched lakes. That is, they sit up there in a basin, surrounded by sandy hills, well above the water table. K'gari has more than half of the world's perched lakes and Boomanjin is the largest such lake in the world, but how can a lake exist in sand well above the water table, I hear you ask? The answer is that a layer of decaying vegetation forms a near impervious layer at the bottom of each lake. The decaying vegetation makes these freshwater lakes very acidic and poor in nutrients, so any creature living in the lake must have adapted to such conditions.

Another interesting feature of the perched lakes is that some have colourless water while others have yellow/brown or reddish water, the result of tannins and other organic chemicals in the water. The variation depends on the type of sand that the water has leached through to form the lake. If the water has leached through yellow/brown sands high in aluminium and iron, then these elements react with the tannins, causing them to precipitate and settle out of the water thus creating a colourless water lake. If, on the other hand, water leaches though white sand devoid of aluminium and iron, no such reaction will occur. The tannins will remain in the water and give it a characteristic tea colour.

Masses of phebalium were in flower everywhere as well as what looked to me like a species of dillwynia and I loved seeing the melaleucas growing by the edge of the lakes.

The perched lakes are superb and fragile ecosystems. Access to them is limited, which is a good thing. To see them is unforgettable.

I bounced around on the sandy road all the way to Dilli village. The former sand mining site is now a private research facility run by USC (University of the Sunshine Coast). From there, I tore along the beach to Eurong, getting up to 100 kph. That was fun and I would have liked to do a bit more but I had to turn off at Eurong to head back to Central Station. I seemed to encounter it in no time at all.

Eurong is a resort of sorts. I didn't stop there but I noticed that it has all the usual kind of stuff: a pub, servo, bakery and accommodation.

My partner and I bounced around again, going from Eurong back to Central Station. There was quite a lot of burning off going on along this stretch of road. Also along the way, some of K'gari's tall trees were labelled. They included scribbly gum, with their characteristic larval 'scribbles' under the bark, blackbutt, tallowwood, pink bloodwood and satinay.

> Mostly tripe
> Is all the hype.
> Talk, talk, talk,
> Don't people love to squawk?
> But sometimes it is real,
> A true and honest deal.
> And there are times, rarer still,
> When words or quill cannot fulfill.
>
> My friends, leave not in a hurry,
> When people talk of K'gari.

Day 37

Today, day thirty-seven, I walked to Lake McKenzie and it was there that my mind was blown away. You hear the hype, of course you do, don't we all? Of K'gari's beaches, forests, dunes, dingoes and…the lakes! But nothing, nothing, prepared me for the majesty of Lake McKenzie. It is a startling azure sapphire set in white gold and I am not talking hype. I will leave it at that. See it for yourself. Swim in its delicious water.

The fourteen-kilometre return walk left me tired but very, very content.

Day 38

I said goodbye to K'gari today but, as I was booked on the five p.m. ferry, I had some time to kill. I killed it by having another look at Lake McKenzie, I simply had to, this time by car. I saw Lake Wabby too, then I spent what remained of the afternoon having a nap and wandering around Kingfisher Resort. It is the usual thing: tennis, bars, bistros and fancy accommodation.

In a word, I got bored and, as is usually the case when I am bored, my mind blew a fuse and proceeded of its own accord into the realm of the weird so, if the reader has had enough of the warped warbles of my deranged thinking, then I suggest that you give the next section, my sandfly rant, a big miss.

I did not see a single termite mound on K'gari. It must be hard for the little termite carpenters to build them out of pure sand. So I surmised that on K'gari, the sandfly must be king and reigns unchallenged, even though I had not sustained a single bite from these ferocious little bloodsuckers on my entire K'gari stopover; no matter, the yarn must go on regardless of facts.

The reader may have noticed that I have two phobias: sandflies and mosquitoes. They exist purely to torment. Why they ever made it onto Noah's Ark still baffles me; most likely as stowaways, I suspect. The intelligent reader will soon realise what they have in common, but it is not just the fact that they suck your blood and leave behind a nasty little calling card that drives you demented for days with itch, but also, and perhaps most distressing of all, that they actively and mercilessly seek you out.

That is where they differ for instance from bees, wasps and spiders, who will without doubt leave you with a nasty bite or sting, but they will generally pay you no mind if you are willing to oblige them to live and let live. Of the two, I find that sandflies are the worst, for me at least. The reaction I get to them is ridiculous, given their size. In fact, you can't even see the sandflies from my neck of the woods but they are there all right, waiting voraciously for a bit of skin. At least mosquitoes can be seen and heard, you mostly know when they are about and can take appropriate steps, but sandflies are the epitome of stealth; almost invisible silent bloodsucking mongrels who are out to getcha.

I take inordinate precautions against both phobia-inducing critters. I will cover every patch of skin I can even on a hot day. You won't see me in shorts, ever, if I am anywhere near them. I don't care if I have to use a litre of chemicals a day to keep them at bay; I will do anything and endure any hardship to prevent a bite. But I still get them. If I let my guard down the tiniest bit, they will pounce and drink with good cheer and laugh at the misery they know will come to me.

I bravely set aside my fears of a dastardly sandfly ambush to visit an island made up entirely of their favourite habitat, for which, methinks, I deserve at the very least a mention in despatches.

While on the island, I had heard talk, rumours, of a certain Mr Fry, apparently a Mr Big in the sandfly world, although his existence is unknown even to Google, which immediately raises severe doubts about the veracity of this so-called Mr Fry, but the talk is too loud to be ignored. Nor is there any information on Google about the sandfly language so I suppose that his name is a human invention and that his true name is unknown. Try Googling sandfly language yourself and all you get is how to do sandfly in sign language.

I have gleaned from all the talk that Mr Fry is Chinese, although some say Japanese and others Indonesian. An American couple insisted most vehemently that anyone so successful must be from the States. A loner, drunk at the bar one night, swore that he was from Port Moresby.

Regardless of his roots, it seems that he was a famous and very successful international spy, something of a James Bond type male sandfly's sandfly, hacking into military and corporate files and running a huge network of agents. He became famous, too famous in fact, for fame is detrimental to the spying business and that, together with almost drowning in one of his own martinis, forced him into early retirement whereupon he became just another mongrel bloodsucking bastard.

But even at that, this ultra-competitive beast had to be the best. He rapidly moved up the rankings, faster than any sandfly had ever done before. He became an ace, and in barely any time at all became the holder of the world record for the highest number of confirmed bites on humans.

As one would expect, his fame soared to ever higher levels and he soon became known the world over and with such fame always comes the opportunity to make serious money. Mr Fry saw to this by opening a chain of flied-food outlets which, in record time, made him the richest sandfly on the planet.

What to do with such a stash of loot has long vexed the human race and it seems that, in that respect, as well as in some other notable ones, sandflies are no different. It is perhaps the greatest worry that afflicts all living things. After many sleepless nights, which was by no means a problem for this sandfly's hyperactive mind, Mr Fry tackled and solved that particular concern in the best way possible, by making even more money, shitloads of it. He achieved his momentous success by buying up big; investing if you wish. He bought K'gari, the entire island, lock, stock and barrel, for a song, as well as every other desirable patch of sand the world over, from Acapulco to Hawaii, the long way around, and created resorts catering to every taste, whim and income. They have the best sand, pools, casinos, bars and accommodation.

His resorts are always bursting at the seams with sandflies by the trillions and they do not share our morality. Males come to eat, get drunk and mate. Females come to tan in banana lounges by the pool, with a cocktail and an easy read, having disposed of the kids in a crèche if it was not possible to leave them at home. They may mate if they choose to or if they get drunk enough, but generally they would prefer to relax unless the opportunity to mate with Mr Fry should come along, for his prowess with the ladies is as legendary as his wealth, power and generosity.

Mr Fry is now a dashing, powerful and filthy rich middle-aged sandfly that all the females would secretly like to mate but very few, only a select few, whose bodies have only just ripened into a beautiful and succulent fruit, get anywhere near the opportunity of fulfilling. He makes males jealous, females envious and rivals murderous, so there have been many attempts on his life but he is too cunning and his security is too good for any to have succeeded. He can outgun, outfight, and outfox any other sandfly anywhere and anytime.

Mr Fry is not excessively vain or narcissistic but only to the moderate extent that his station in life demands, and that is only to be expected, when doors never slam in his face, males grovel at his feet, females throw their charms at him and not a word of his is ever unheard or unheeded. It is compulsory to read his autobiography whenever staying on one of his properties and, given that he owns virtually all the best habitable sand on the planet, very few haven't read it. Failure to do so is punishable by death; fair enough too. But why wouldn't a sandfly read it? It has everything a red-blood-filled sandfly could possibly want: intrigue, graphic sexual exploits, violence, killing and tips on how to become a success. As a work, it is universally admired and adored, published in a thousand sandfly dialects, and is even available as an audio for the illiterate and the blind.

They say that Mr Fry has fifty mansions; sprawling, multi-storey affairs made of the best quality sand, each with its own gym, pool, golf course, yacht and luxury cars – one car for each week of the year and he spends the other two looking for something new in cars.

Is he happy? What sort of question is that? Of course he is. Why wouldn't he be? The word is that Mr Fry, ex international spy, prize bloodsucker, charismatic entrepreneur, fast-food magnate, the biggest of big-time property developers, philanthropist (yes, he gives sand to the needy in generous quantities and with only a tasteful amount of publicity) and, last but by no means least, fabulous lover, has a harem ten million strong and has fathered in excess of half a trillion little blighters that he has nothing at all to do with. Joy of joys.

Yes indeed, his resorts are happy places where males sit at the bar and drink and perve and wait for an opportunity; and females in bikinis adjust their sunglasses and wait for an opportunity. What are they waiting for? The next meals-on-wheels to come along and me in particular.

I wish to advise that, after all that rubbish, we now resume normal programming.

I found a rough patch of bush in which to camp, just on dark, not far out of River Heads. I was just off the main road that takes you from River Heads to either Maryborough or Harvey Bay, so the traffic noise next morning was considerable, but not enough to ruin the glorious song of the grey shrike-thrush that serenaded me for a while. I made for Tin Can Bay; another place I had heard spoken of with much favour.

Day 39

I skirted Maryborough, situated on the Mary River, and I was impressed by the little part of it I saw. Doubtless, I saw the top end of town where dosh in abundance resides, but the beautifully restored Queenslander houses around St Mary's School were something to behold. The local shopping precinct was well done too, with an understated old world feel to it; but I didn't stop for a closer inspection as there was nothing I needed and shops aren't my thing.

The Mary River seems to mark the southern extent of the crocodile domain, so from here on in, the only large chompers one need worry about are of the shark variety, but, alas, the climate was getting colder and the sea correspondingly less tempting so, there you go, you can't win.

Tin Can Bay is a delightful spot and has the makings of a worthy place to spend a week or so. It is just the right size and not over-developed. The waterways are superb and must be great for boating and fishing. It has beautiful parks, a great foreshore walk, much birdlife and diesel at 199.9 c/l.

I did a long section of the foreshore walk, starting at the yacht club, and passed through mangrove, she-oak, cypress pine and eucalypt woodland. It was the usual muddy sand estuarine habitat. The birds were prolific and their cacophony astounding, especially from the lorikeets and noisy miners, and the signage along the way describing the different birds to be found in the area was excellent.

One thing perplexed me, the section of raised boardwalk that is wide enough to drive a truck along, with a wide load, on a surface far better than the Newell's what's more. I am not sure what they are expecting! Herds of ornithologists perhaps, stampeding to get to a rare sighting: pushing, elbowing, kicking and gouging to get there first.

Doubtless, if such a thing was ever to occur, a wide walkway would save the lives of many ornithologists from being crushed to death. Shire money well spent, I should think, for the world would be a sadder place with less ornithologists.

It was a short drive from Tin Can Bay to Rainbow Beach and what a sight awaited me there. The town is just another seaside town but a bit more touristy and alive than most other small towns I had seen so far. I walked south along the beach, and yes, I know, another beach walk, but this one was different and by that I don't mean the car that got stuck on rocks trying to escape the rising tide nor, for that matter, the sea; I mean the dunes.

The dunes, the dunes, the glorious dunes; my goodness, I've never seen anything like it. The colours of the sand are worthy of the palette of Van Gogh or Rembrandt: red, orange, white, cream, black, tan and brown. I could not quite believe what my eyes were telling me. Such an extraordinary range of colours of sand, in the one place, seemed impossible to me. Surely my brain had had some sort of psychedelic meltdown and tripped out on me but no, I looked and looked again, and the colours remained. I touched the different sands and the colours did not fade away or blend to an inept beige.

As I mentioned previously, it is a wondrous gift to be amazed; perhaps the best gift one can receive, next to love. Maybe love is to be amazed. Anyway, you, the reader, have not paid good money to read me philosophising about love so I will get back to what I am supposed to be focused on and what you, I hope, want to read about.

Damn it, but I fiercely regretted not having any containers to take some samples of the sand with me to amaze those back home. To produce small multicoloured packets of amazement as gifts. What one could do with all those colours; and to think that here too, between 1965 and 1976, sand was mined, mostly for titanium, I believe. Is nothing sacred? And yet, wasn't I wishing to mine a little of the sand for my own greedy self just a moment ago? We humans do hypocrisy very well and though I try to keep my level of hypocrisy to a minimum, I do not always succeed.

I visited the Bymien Picnic Area just out of Rainbow Beach in the Great Sandy National Park. The short walk from the picnic ground was pleasant, with the forest very similar to that of K'gari, and would be the next best thing if you cannot get to the island. It was good to see rainforest and tall kauri again. I would have loved to do the walk to Lake Poona but daylight was on the wane.

After a brief stop at Seary's Creek to see the waterholes, with their reddish tea-coloured waters, came the time to resume the regular struggle to find somewhere to rest my weary bones for the night. It was a real drag but I found one not too far further along the road down a sandy track. I quickly came to a gate barring further progress so I simply stayed put there, on the road, before the gate, on the right side of the law, and amongst flowering heathland.

Day 40

Day forty was miserable – raining and cold. Unfortunately, not an ideal day to visit Noosa. I had never been to Noosa and I was looking forward to seeing the place even though I expected it to be very developed. I finally arrived at Noosa Heads but I was in a somewhat exasperated and bewildered state after the confusion of so many roundabouts and signs. I'm sure I went the long way around to get there but who cares? It is a pretty spot, just as I had heard, where the Noosa River reaches the sea. The beach is beautiful and the sand was more like what I am used to on a beach. I cursed the weather gods for ruining the day; no more crocs to worry about, finally, but now it was freezing. In my book, it was far too cold for a swim. All I could do was walk around, imagine what might have been, and piss off.

I stopped for the night at Eumundi, an RV friendly town, on some open ground near the tennis club and toilet block. I spent what was left of this forgettable day finishing *Vanity Fair* and commencing *The Father of Forensics*, by Colin Evans, another op-shop treasure which tells the interesting story of Sir Bernard Spilsbury and his pioneering work on forensics and the investigation of crime scenes. It was fascinating. If you ever find it, grab it.

I had never heard of the Eumundi Market until a message from my niece rectified this inadequacy and, if the weather gods had pissed on me, at least now came some recompense from the market gods because the market would be open the next day, Saturday.

Day 41

Let me warn anyone as ignorant as myself; the Eumundi Market is huge and it is crowded and you must get there early if you don't want to have to park nearer to Brisbane than Eumundi.

I spent a couple of hours wandering around the market in a daze. I can see the appeal but it wasn't my thing. One coffee was enough for me. Everywhere you turned, every lane you went down, every stall you passed, there was food, more food, food to get fat on, and stuff, mostly women's stuff, not my kind of stuff. I can say I have been there but that is about all there was in it for me.

That afternoon, I spent a pleasant few hours with a former work colleague at her house at Belli Park, then I was meant to have dinner with some friends at Noosa but that fell through, so I ended up spending the night somewhere between Belli Park and Kenilworth, once more on a dismal little side road amongst a little mangy bushland. It wasn't paradise, you could toss a coin to the main road, but it was somewhere to sleep.

Day 42

Next morning, as I was breakfasting, I was on the receiving end of an outrageous insult. It reminded me of the time, only a few years ago, when, for the first time, someone offered me their seat in a tram. It was a nice gesture, well-meant, but it came as a shock. I politely declined the young man's offer and I realised that to him, in his twenties I would say, I was an old man. I was sixty, and sure, the grey hair, the grey beard, the bald head and the sagging corners of the mouth all make me look older, no doubt about it, but the thing is, I don't feel old. What I see in the mirror surprises me and I know a lot of people the same age as me, men and women, who feel the same way. Age sneaks up on you, uninvited, in a way that seems to make one age physically well ahead of mentally.

Anyway, I was mucking around getting breakfast ready, or finishing up, I can't remember which, and you need to understand a bit about the set-up I had for feeding myself which I alluded to earlier in this work but which the reader may have forgotten by now. Rolling up the sides of the canvas canopy revealed, on one side, my cooking arrangement; a nine-kilogram gas bottle with a single burner and, on the other side, the side facing the road on this occasion, a two-door cupboard lying on its side with two compartments, one full of food and the other full of utensils, pots and pans. It was a good set-up, just the way I like things, organised and efficient so that I needn't waste time searching for anything.

So my camp spot was visible from the main road on this particular day, my forty-second. There happened to be a cycling event on. Cyclists went past at frequent intervals in ones and twos or in small groups. They joined my road at a T-intersection barely a hundred or so metres away from me where police were in attendance to ensure their safety. Some of the cyclists went past me chatting, some were silent, others laughed and none of them seemed to be slogging away too hard. I expect that the sloggers would have passed through much earlier.

'Look at the old man's set-up,' I heard one say. 'Not bad,' the other replied.

I looked up from what I was doing, feeling affronted, only to catch a brief glimpse of two young men cycling past, talking amiably with smiles on their faces where they should have been focused on their cycling and sporting grimaces of pain instead. Old man? Old man, they reckon! Hmmpf. But of course to them, no older than in their mid-twenties, that's exactly what I was. It briefly unsettled me and then I laughed out loud to myself. I'll get used to it in time.

It was a nice drive from where I was to Maleny; the highlight being, without a doubt, Kenilworth's designer dunny. It is the grandest and most bombastic dunny I have ever seen and if not already World Heritage listed, then it bloody well should be. It is contemporary art fused with ancient Australian culture fused with an eye-catching tourist attraction fused with a place to take a dump. It is simply gob-smackingly unique.

It is meant to portray a basket, and I get that, but it reminds me more of a fireworks display with bright yellow, blue and orange-brown colours and sprays of white reaching upward. The white tentacles, reaching for the heavens, have a spiritual intensity about them which may even serve to sanctify the unsavoury processes occurring within. Seeing it, you can't help but smile and feel good, and what more could the people who designed and built the thing ask for? I dips me lid to the lot of them. I only hope that it never gets graffitied on and that it comes with genuine Aussie redbacks.

I regret not going inside but neither bladder nor bowel compelled me to. I should have anyway and I will regret not seeing the inside of the Kenilworth dunny to my dying day.

Maleny was a disappointment to me. I had heard comparisons made of Maleny with a small town I used to live near in Victoria called Yackandandah but it is nothing like 'Yack' (as the locals call it); Yackandandah is much smaller and far more charming. To be fair, I didn't stop in Maleny, for I was still on a high from seeing the Kenilworth dunny, but from what I could see cruising through, apart from some boutique shops and the usual array of cafés, I found Maleny to be bustling, commercial and just another mid-size rural town. It had a large Woolies and other big shops which Yackandandah doesn't have and which detracted from what I had expected, arising from what I had heard.

Somewhere and at some time, I got onto Steve Irwin Way and drove past Australia Zoo but I didn't stop there as I wanted to go to the Glass House Mountains. Those remarkable mountains that simply jut out of the surrounding plains were irresistible to me. I felt their attractive pull more and more the closer I got, inversely proportional to the square of the radius, and once there, there were so many options to explore that I was almost driven to despair.

I chose to do the four-kilometre circuit walk around the base of Mt Tibrogargan, which gave me a taste of the terrain, but, to my eternal shame, I did not attempt the very steep and rugged ascent to the summit as I didn't have the right footwear. (Not an excuse but a rationally thought-out reason.)

Named by, you guessed it, surely, James Cook; these mountains are intrusive plugs formed by volcanic activity about twenty-six million years ago. Lava hardened within the vent of a number of volcanoes and over millions of years, as the softer surrounding rock eroded away, the durable plugs remained to form the mountains we see today. They reminded me of the Warrumbungles, which were formed by the same process, and they are a walker's, nature lover's, rock climber's and abseiler's dream.

After the walk, I left, feeling happy and with a couple of the best tasting pineapples you could imagine, cheap too, direct from the farmer, bless him, bought at his little stall at the Tibrogargan car park. I made for Caboolture, where I planned to stay at a friend's place for a few nights of R and R. The usual thing: get clean, wash some clothes, reconnect with humans, as well as using it as a base to explore Brisbane as I had never spent time there, merely passed through.

I made one more stop along the way, out of curiosity, at a small park near Beerburrum that I was surprised to see was called Matthew Flinders Park. Yes indeed, Lieutenant Matthew Flinders RN, the one and only, even made it to this place, on 26 July 1799. The plaque in the park commemorating his inland journey here from his ship, the *Norfolk*, quotes from his journal entry:

> ...a stream of water induced us to stop for the night, the sun being then below the trees. At seven in the morning we were under the steep cliffs of the flat topped peak...the steepness of the cliffs, utterly forbad all idea of ascending to the top...

The plaque goes on to explain,

> Having already climbed Mt. Beerburrum, it is near this site that on 26 July 1799 Lt. Matthew Flinders RN, together with his Aboriginal guide Bongaree and two seamen, camped overnight by Tibrogargan Creek. The group had also intended to climb Mt. Tibrogargan but upon viewing its steepness, returned instead to Flinders' ship the Norfolk.

It was yet another curious piece of history that I found dotted about in my travels and which I find so fascinating.

I spent six nights in Caboolture and thoroughly enjoyed my time there with my friend Robyn and her sister Jan, in Jan's house. There was good food, plenty of it, good drink, too much at times, laughs, music, some dancing, movie watching and seeing some sights. I was looking forward to seeing a bit of Brisbane and its surrounds, the experience to be so much the better with the benefit of enthusiastic local knowledge. I repaid my hosts' kindness by busying myself in the miserable garden, which was a shambles by any standards, and redoing their abysmal vegie patch.

Day 43–Day 47

Day one in Caboolture was a quiet one after a morning walk. On day two, we went to Bribie Island, which was a mixed bag. The sun was out and we had the fortune of a gloriously warm day. We found a beach that we had to ourselves and decided to do a spot of fishing. My track record as an angler is a very poor one. I am of the strong opinion that my fingertips secrete and impart onto the hook and bait some form of fish-repelling chemical. The fish rarely get hooked; they simply nibble, find it distasteful and flee.

Robyn had brought along a couple of handlines and, as predictable as a plot in a B-grade movie, Robyn caught a fish and I caught bugger-all. She landed a good-size gummy shark, at least that's what Robyn thought it was, I wouldn't know, but it was a beautiful creature that none of us could bring ourselves to kill so we let the fillets of flake return to the sea for someone with less scruples to fry.

Not catching fish doesn't bother me any more. I have accepted it as the natural order. Perhaps the fish sense my pessimism through the quivering of the line and the timbre of the hook and in the sourness it imparts to the bait and duly oblige to perpetuate my defeatist attitude forevermore. Anyway, whatever the reason may be, I love eating fish but I am not so keen to be the one killing them these days, so I'm more than happy to leave the killing to others.

So my lack of success bothered me not. My failure to prove myself a manly hunter in front of the women bothered me not. That a woman caught a fish and I didn't bothered me not. What did bother me, and the ladies, is that a pleasant day was ruined by a most unpleasant dinner.

One would think, or at least we thought, that on Bribie Island you would get a decent feed of fish and chips, or at least even half decent, but unfortunately the feed we copped that evening wasn't even one sixty-fourth decent; it was thoroughly indecent. We were in agreement that it was the worst fish and chips any of us had ever had. The food was so oily that you might as well have drunk oil straight from the bottle and somehow they managed to serve up the calamari rings all glued together in a single blob. It was awful. We should have sent it back but none of us could be bothered. Our loss soon became the gain of the scavenging ibis that hung around the place and I could see why so many of them hung about for, judging by the quality of the food on offer, I'd say that the birds were very well fed and most certainly a little on the plump side.

Day three was a ripper. We went to Redcliffe and saw the Bee Gees Way. I'm a fan and I knew they had spent some time in Australia after the family emigrated from England but I didn't know where so the memorial laneway came as a complete surprise to me. Unveiled in 2013, it is informative, very well put together, and a fitting tribute to the group. When barely in their teens, it is here that the brothers' musical career started as they landed a regular gig singing from the back of a truck in between races at the Redcliffe Speedway, with appreciative people in the crowd throwing money onto the track. Redcliffe is also where the Bee Gees signed their first musical contract way back in 1958. Their songs played continuously and I couldn't resist having my photo taken with the life-size statues of the group both as children and as adults.

Day four was just as good. We took the Brisbane River ferry from Brett's Wharf at Hamilton, upstream, past Brisbane's CBD, disembarking at Southbank. The forty-minute trip was a great way to see the riverside scenery, old and new mansions and the many old brick warehouses and wool stores.

Hamilton, incidentally, is where the pioneer aviator, Charles Kingsford-Smith, was born in 1897. After living for a while in Canada, the remarkable man spent most of his youth growing up in Sydney. He enlisted in the 1st AIF in 1915 and served at Gallipoli before transferring across to the Royal Flying Corps, serving with distinction before being shot down in 1917. Recovering from his wounds, he returned as a flight instructor and with flight well and truly in his soul.

In 1928, he and three others made the first trans-Pacific flight, aboard the *Southern Cross,* from California to Brisbane, with stops at Hawaii and Fiji. Later the same year, he made the first non-stop flight across Australia from Melbourne to Perth and the first trans-Tasman flight from Sydney to Christchurch.

In 1930, he made a trans-Atlantic crossing from Ireland to Newfoundland, having just had the *Southern Cross* refurbished in the Netherlands and, later that year, he competed in and won an England to Australia air race.

In 1935, while attempting to break the England–Australia air speed record in the *Lady Southern Cross,* Kingsford-Smith and his co-pilot, John Pethybridge, disappeared over the Andaman Sea and their bodies were never recovered. As the old cliché goes, Kingsford-Smith, a great Australian, died doing what he loved. It is a comforting thought and I hope that Pethybridge loved flying just as much as 'Smithy' and that both men made their final flight on gossamer wings.

At Southbank, we met up with Jenny and her sister Glenda, for lunch. Jenny, whose son's house in Calliope I observed to be indeed a house, Robyn and I share some history, with the common denominator being a caravan park in good ol' Vic. Jenny and her partner at the time ran the caravan park, Robyn stayed there for about six months while meandering about in her clapped-out bus and I stayed there for almost two years as I waited for construction to get going on my block at Port Albert. Everything but time and the wind happens slowly in Port Albert.

It was a most pleasant afternoon we all spent together. I felt like a rooster amongst a harem of four old chooks (joke), each more stunning than the one before (sort of joke). The gardens at Southbank are superb, much of them being a recreation of the rainforest Queensland is famous for. We had a nice lunch, I can't remember where, and no sooner had we left our table than the ubiquitous ibis came to remove the scraps. After a stroll, we had coffee and chocolates elsewhere, inside and closed off to ibis or I am sure they would have joined us again.

I wouldn't hesitate to recommend Brisbane's Southbank for a day out, especially if going there by boat.

Day 48

I left Caboolture on day forty-eight once I got the flat battery seen to by the RACQ. Clearly, my partner did not want to leave and I couldn't blame her. I had a great time there and the hospitality was relaxed and impeccable with only the occasional squabble between the two sisters. I went, having added a stash of good memories to my over-crowded hippocampus.

I spent my final night in Queensland, not for ever I hope, in the home of Glenda and her husband John, together with Jenny and their two greyhounds, Jesse and Elli. They live in Birkdale, a suburb of Brisbane, on half an acre of beautiful garden. Glenda is a plant and garden freak, just like someone else I know, so we had much to talk about. John keeps bees which produce a most exquisite honey.

We took the greyhounds for a walk in the evening, along with a neighbour's dog who has the unfortunate but well-deserved nickname of 'Shitty'. He never fails to produce at least three deposits per walk and his record is seven. On this particular evening, he only managed a miserly four, so I suggested that he might need some Metamucil, a laxative I am well acquainted with thanks to a very good friend of mine in Melbourne who takes it every day with a smile and swears that it, and it alone, keeps him alive.

Day 49

So on day forty-nine I said goodbye to Queensland, with a couple of pots of honey, and hello again to New South Wales. Having seen the northernmost point of the mainland, I now made for the easternmost.

I reached Byron Bay in the afternoon but I didn't stop in the town, as the slums were too much for me. I saw paupers peddle their miserable wares for a few cents and cunning Dickensian urchins begging for a coin or two while being alert for an opportunity to pick a pocket or to snatch a bag. Besides, the town didn't enchant me; it was the cape and the lighthouse I wanted to see while plentiful daylight remained.

The lighthouse and the adjacent keepers' cottages were built in 1901 and the planners back then lacked the foresight to include a decent car park so, finding nowhere to park up there, I walked from a picnic ground that I cannot remember the name of, up to the spectacular and rather grand Cape Byron lighthouse. The setting, and the steps leading up to the lighthouse, are imposing and the entrance to the lighthouse itself, with its ornate wooden door, would not be out of place on a Victorian mansion.

Naturally, I made my way to the very tip of the cape, where I paused for some time, watching the waves crashing onto the rocks, getting drenched by one, and collecting some stones of the most easterly variety before retreating from the tide that was clearly rising.

Cape Byron was named by, guess who, James Cook in 1770. Its name has nothing to do with the poet, who wasn't born until 1788, but was named after a British explorer, John Byron, who, aboard HMS *Dolphin*, circumnavigated the globe from 1764 to 1766. Lord Byron, the poet, was his illustrious grandson.

Day 50

I stopped for the night near Ballina and the following day I decided to visit Iluka, at the mouth of the Clarence River. It was a fortuitous decision because the small hamlet was very much to my liking and, more importantly, I got to see the adjacent national park, which is World Heritage listed, is the largest remnant littoral (coastal) rainforest in NSW and which I had no idea existed. So, for me, it was an exciting find.

I did the 5.5-kilometre return walk to Iluka Bluff, experiencing the wonderful rainforest all the way. There were many vines, ferns and strangler figs. The bird life was exciting too. As well as the usual platoon of brush turkeys scratching around, I saw an eastern yellow robin, a green-winged pigeon and a stunningly beautiful blue-faced honeyeater which came to withing a couple of metres of me as I rested perfectly still under a pandanus palm. Oh, and I heard a whipbird, but how often do you get to see them?

From Iluka, I proceeded to Sawtell, noticing along the way that the sugar cane plantations had finally petered out around Grafton, having accompanied me down the east coast from Mossman. That is a lot of sugar and a hell of a lot of calories or, I should say, kilojoules.

Sawtell is a charming coastal town just south of Coffs Harbour, on Bonville Creek, and the walk out to Bonville Head Lookout is superb, with fantastic views. It is also very exposed and the stiff onshore wind kept threatening to blow me to Kempsey. It is worth going beyond the lookout to get to Bongil Beach, an enticing beach which I would normally get thrilled by. However, by this time, I was well beyond being thrilled by a beach or enticed to walk along one so, after a bit of a poke around, I turned back.

I spent the night at the entrance to Bongil Bongil National Park, just out of Sawtell, with the intention of doing a walk in the park next morning.

Day 51

The 4.6-kilometre return walk to the Bongil Picnic Area was well worth the time and effort. The picnic area is sublimely situated on the bank of Bonville Creek, which here has the dimensions of a river. The platform over the creek gives you a taste of the thick forest on each bank and it must be a delight to canoe the creek from here all the way to the sea. What a special adventure that would be through a stretch of what I imagine would be largely pristine country. I recall walking through a laneway flanked by tall melaleucas with extraordinary sheets of papery bark and also seeing the delightful wedding bush, *Ricinocarpus pinifolius*, in flower. It has vivid white flowers that always excite me when I see them and they never fail to bring a smile to my face and, unlike its namesake, the bush usually doesn't turn to excrement in the end; compost perhaps, but not shit.

By this time, I felt that I had been away from home for long enough and I had been mostly on my own for long enough and that I had seen enough. I was missing those familiar things, the full gamut: people, animals, plants and places. It was time to go home.

To that end, I took the express home, stopping only to sleep. The weather turning to rain and hail from Newcastle southward helped my cause. Having left Bongil Bongil National Park, I bypassed Newcastle and the congestion of Sydney, picked up the M31 and stopped for the night in a treed park just out of Berrima.

Nature's refrigeration worked very well that night. There was frost on the ground and almost frost on my ears and nose the following morning, day fifty-two, but the sky was crystal clear and a fresh blue.

Day 52

I left early as I was very keen to get the car heater cranked up. The old girl feels the cold every bit as much as I do these days and she did her usual coughing and spluttering, like an early morning smoker's cough, before she fired up.

I stopped at Jugiong reserve for brunch and later, with the fine weather making me more inclined to stop and sightsee, I decided to look at the thing we've all heard about but which I have never seen, the old Dog on the Tuckerbox at Gundagai. I had only the vaguest notion of what it is about, the old story about a dog guarding his owner's tuckerbox and, whether the story is apocryphal or not, that seems to be about all there is to it. The whole concept seems to derive from a poem called 'Bill the Bullocky', published in 1857 or 1880 under the name of Bowyang York, which seems to be a fictitious name. It refers to a dog sitting in the tuckerbox five miles from Gundagai, rather than on the tuckerbox, which seems a bit odd. Anyway, it all took off from there and I guess it brought a measure of fame, tourism, and business to Gundagai.

The statue, unveiled in 1932, is a simple one; simple and yet powerful. It depicts a dog, that looks like a kelpie to me, sitting on a tuckerbox labelled *tuckerbox*. You wonder what all the fuss is about and just how it captured the imagination of a nation so. I suppose it reflects our love of dogs and their love of us, their loyalty, which we cherish, and the romanticism of the old pioneering and droving days and its association with the companionship of mates, horses and dogs. Although money seems to come second to none nowadays, perhaps always, the statue of a dog on a box is a reminder that love and loyalty have a prominent place in our deep psyche.

Next stop was at another place I have driven past a dozen times but, I'm somewhat ashamed to say, never bothered to stop at and that is the Australian Truck Drivers' Memorial in Tarcutta. It is described as a sacred memorial dedicated to the truck drivers and associated workers who have lost their lives in the line of duty in the transport industry, in the same way as memorials are dedicated to fallen soldiers or police. Tarcutta was chosen because of its situation on the Hume Highway, halfway between Melbourne and Sydney. To see the lists of names of all those that have died over the years is very moving. There is a service held annually at the memorial in October.

I stopped briefly at HMAS *Otway*, the submarine at Holbrook, for old time's sake. We had stopped there a few times when the kids were little in what seems now, through a nostalgic lens, a remnant of happy times.

The *Otway* was an Oberon class submarine of the Royal Australian Navy commissioned in 1968 and decommissioned in 1994. It appears that she never saw active service but has the glory of being the first RAN vessel to visit Ghana and the first to round the Cape of Good Hope.

Finally, on this day of brief encounters, I stopped at Wodonga, part of my old stomping ground. I couldn't help feeling a little emotional as things from the past came back to me. I got some fish and chips at a shop on the main drag and as I walked along I happened to notice a commemorative display on the dreadful 2019–2020 bushfires.

The unprecedented fires across NSW and Victoria began in July 2019, in winter, and continued until March 2020, destroyed over 5.4 million hectares of land and 2,000 homes in NSW and 1.2 million hectares in Victoria. It is estimated that one billion animals perished. The display includes enlarged photos as well as audio commentary which can be accessed online. It pays a fitting tribute to all the firefighters and support staff who risked their lives and gave up their time in this hour of great need. The fires even managed to turn back our PM at the time from his Hawaiian holiday, eventually.

For the final time, I managed to eke out a camp for the night, just, in some overgrown scrub where the Kiewa Valley Highway crosses Yackandandah Creek. Tomorrow, I had some people I wanted to meet, then I would be back in Melbourne.

Day 53

The following day I went to Tangambalanga, a small but growing town in the Kiewa valley, where I once worked. Its extraordinary name, but not as good as Murrumbidgee, is thought to be derived from an Aboriginal word for the Murray River or white-clawed lobster. I love some of those Aboriginal names: long, and they roll around in your mouth like a lolly.

First of all, I visited someone who is a former 'many things': butcher, patient of mine and helper on my farm, but he is not a former friend because we have remained friends. We don't communicate often, he is that type of friend, but it's a pleasure when we do and it's generally to discuss the success or otherwise of our beloved Geelong Cats. We talked over a coffee of the usual things: kids, what we'd been up to, my trip, and our hope that the Cats might add another premiership to their collection.

Next, I caught up with John and Chloris, also in Tangambalanga and also former patients of mine. We share a love of plants. John is passionate about native orchids and he has a wonderful collection and I did further and considerable damage to the holiday budget by buying some that I had to have. Chloris loves all plants and photographing them. She very kindly gave me some of her hoyas.

John and Chloris had recently returned from a trip to the Simpson Desert. We talked for a while about our respective journeys and it sounded like theirs was a lot rougher than mine in terms of road conditions, which, for me, took the gloss off their strong recommendation to do the trip myself.

Finally, I had lunch in Myrtleford, the last town I worked in before retiring, at the ever-welcoming home of George and Linda; oh, and

Bella, their old dog. George is Italian and Linda is an Aussie, they met while working on a tobacco farm and they have been married a long time. The food was laid on thick, as usual, and it went down with no trouble at all, as usual.

Three hours after leaving Myrtleford, I was back in Melbourne, at my sister's house. Fifty-three days, 11,272 kilometres and just over $3,000-worth of diesel later. The trip to the tip was worth every day, every K and every dollar.

Home

The Wizard

A change takes place.
The strange brew bubbles.
It must not burn
Lest its power diminish.

The magic must be nurtured
Or its vapours made toxic,
To affect all
And all to be lessened.

The wizard keeps to his task,
His best or not,
Causing life to the un-life
And more than is conceivable.

It promises not,
Endless summers;
Solely the chance
To keep winter's clutch at bay.

The wizard knows the craft
That mortals cannot fathom; ever.
But the miracle he gives chance to
Takes more than mere enchantment.

'Tis forever
A work unfinished.
A bit of this, a bit of that.
More of this, less of another.

The brew bubbles,
Bringing breath's mist to the glass,
A creaking of boards,
The slam of a door.

'Tis no trouble at all
To stir up a curled cat, a scratching dog,
And the hum
Of myriad sounds of those born to die.

The lid dances to a rhythm,
Glorifying love's conception.
And in three quarter
All that matters is come.

Time matters not to him.
He has all he needs and surplus.
To add patters to thumps
And an impatient run to calm steps.

But it is a trap
To consider the potion infallible.
The wizard knows too well
That it is not.

> He adds laughter to balance tears;
> Stirs, nurtures, and prays.
> But failure stares back when he looks deeply
> For a lasting ingredient he cannot conjure.

After a few nights in Melbourne for post-expedition catch-ups and the telling of tales, it was time to go home to Port Albert. I had only lived there for two months but I had been out that way for a couple of years so it did feel like home. To me, it represented a picking up of pieces and a fresh start.

It got me thinking about what home means: something different for each of us, I suspect, and yet, home must share some universal features we all identify with. For me, it is essential that I have a home of my own where I can do whatever I want whenever I want, within the constraints imposed by myself and society of course. Even when we are apart, my home and I are inseparable. Home is a place to be missed and I always miss it sooner or later. It is a place you know will always be there and that you will return to. It is a place of comfort, familiarity and safety.

I went home, back to my beloved plants and garden, back to the dogs and people I had missed, back to living in my shed in a measure of comfort until the house is built, back to tasks and getting the house built and the fulfilment of progress, back to where I finally have power in the shed to make life much easier in this day and age, back to getting on top of the weeds once more, back for the start of spring and getting the vegies going, back for the start of the footy finals, back to unpacking and cleaning, back to getting my partner serviced and cleaned, and her wounds seen to, back to my writing, back to walking around the town and the bush tracks, clearing weeds and picking up rubbish as I go along, back to this small coastal town in southern Victoria and the cold, rain and incessant wind that is spring in these parts. It is good to be home. Home!

Epilogue

I thought for a long time about my top three destinations –; not what they were, for I found that quite easy, but in what order to put them. To rank them was the hard part, so until now I have simply rattled them off for people and said that they are in no particular order. But the ranking of them wouldn't go away, it seemed a cop-out not to, and it became a case of mental gymnastics to get it done.

I am fully aware that what I may consider to be the top three destinations and in what sequence is completely irrelevant to anyone else but it has been for me an exercise of the intellect to rise to the challenge.

So, drum roll, in third place, Cooktown, for all the reasons I have mentioned in the book.

It is the next two I have great trouble ranking and have pondered reasons for some time. You probably have guessed what they are and they could go either way but I have forced myself into a corner and forced myself to make a decision so, here goes.

In second place, Carnarvon Gorge. I absolutely loved the place for its sublime natural beauty. I have a fascination with gorges, rivers, cliffs and the outstanding vegetation and wildlife that goes with such oases. There were several unique natural wonders as well as superb Aboriginal art that could so easily have given it the gold medal.

First place I gave to K'gari. It has a gamut of unique features and unique experiences. It is the largest sand island in the world, it has the most and the largest perched lakes in the world, and it is rightly World Heritage listed. Its forests, pockets of rainforest, creeks, beaches and sandy roads are all breathtaking but it is the lakes, and Lake McKenzie in particular, that quite simply staggered me.

So, after all that, I leave on this note: was utopia found? Well, the answer is, almost.

Utopia implies to me of being in a state of freedom, fulfillment and happiness as well as in a place of natural beauty. There was certainly much of that but not entirely. My main objective was achieved with a minimum of drama but the wilderness experiences I craved were not forthcoming. There was also the ongoing frustration of trying to find somewhere to park my arse for the night. Free camping is very limited but there seems to be no limit to the number of do not enter, entry prohibited, trespassers prosecuted, no camping, permit required, and twenty-four hour video surveillance signs. It makes it hard for the vagabond drifter on a tight budget to explore our land.

Finally, in my opinion, a true utopia is one that is shared with another person, a like-minded person, and only then can utopia be found.

www.ingramcontent.com/pod-product-compliance
Lightning Source LLC
Chambersburg PA
CBHW021105080526
44587CB00010B/384